CREATING A GARDEN
FOR EVERY SEASON

CREATING A GARDEN
FOR EVERY SEASON

The best plants for spring, summer, autumn and winter displays, with over 300 photographs

RICHARD ROSENFELD

southwater

This edition is published by Southwater
an imprint of Anness Publishing Ltd
Blaby Road, Wigston
Leicestershire LE18 4SE
info@anness.com

www.southwaterbooks.com
www.annesspublishing.com

If you like the images in this book and would like to investigate
using them for publishing, promotions or advertising, please visit
our website www.practicalpictures.com for more information.

A CIP catalogue record for this book
is available from the British Library.

Publisher: Joanna Lorenz
Additional text: Kathy Brown, Peter McHoy and Andrew Mikolajski
Designer: WhiteLight
Photographers: Peter Anderson, Jonathan Buckley,
    Sarah Cuttle, John Freeman, Michelle Garrett,
    Debbie Patterson and Steven Wooster
Production Controller: Mai-Ling Collyer

Previously published in four separate volumes, *The Spring Garden*,
The Summer Garden, *The Autumn Garden* and *The Winter Garden*

NOTES
In the directory sections of this book, each plant is given
a hardiness rating. The temperature ranges are as follows:

frost tender – may be damaged by temperatures below 5°C (41°F);
half-hardy – can withstand temperatures down to 0°C (32°F);
frost hardy – can withstand temperatures down to -5°C (23°F);
fully hardy – can withstand temperatures down to -15°C (5°F).

In the United States, throughout the Sun Belt states, from Florida,
across the Gulf Coast, south Texas, southern deserts to Southern
California and coastal regions, annuals are planted in the autumn,
bloom in the winter and spring, and die at the beginning of summer.

CONTENTS

Introduction 6

introduction

ONE OF THE GREAT JOYS OF GARDENING IS the way it puts us in touch with the seasons. In towns and cities it is all too easy nowadays to live from one year to the next with hardly any awareness of the changes in the natural world, except at the most basic level of noticing when we need warm clothes, heating or air-conditioning. As soon as we start gardening, though, a whole new world is opened up, with constantly changing highlights and moments of interest.

Since plants change so dramatically through the year, it is important to think about each season when planning your garden. Winter, especially, is the time that gardeners often forget to plan for –

most plants are dormant, so the range of varieties that are exciting at this time is more limited than for other seasons. But within this somewhat narrower range, there is still a good choice of plants that can make the garden in winter look just as beautiful as during the more showy and colourful growing season. Even during the warmer months careful planning is important, to ensure that you have a continuous display of flowering plants.

For many gardeners, the quiet transition from winter to spring is the most joyous time in the year, symbolizing new life and bringing the promise of all the glories of spring and summer. Early bulbs, such as snowdrops, crocuses and daffodils, signal this new beginning, and a whole series of later-flowering bulbs take over throughout spring and early summer. There are also some wonderful shrubs, such as forsythia, as well as blossom trees, that brighten up the early spring.

For the warmer months, there is an over-whelming range of annuals and perennials that enable you to create whatever effect you choose, whether brilliantly colourful or more delicate and

subdued. Many of these, especially the popular tender perennials and annuals used as bedding plants, such as lobelia and pelargoniums, will flower constantly until hit by the first frosts. Hardy fuchsias, and some roses, flower throughout summer, while most shrubs and climbers have a briefer flowering period so need to be planned for more carefully.

Autumn still boasts many colourful flowers – rudbeckias, chrysanthemums and brilliant dahlias – then, as the cold sets in, other elements take over. Dramatic autumn foliage can be as striking as any summer display, and then there are berries, fruits and seedheads, coloured bark, and the underlying form and structure of leafless trees, as well as shapely evergreens and topiary.

With the help of this book, you can create your perfect garden. You will find here a range of different design ideas, as well as lists of seasonal tasks and space to record your gardening successes and failures. Most important of all, you will find a wonderful selection of plants that will guarantee your garden looks beautiful right through the year.

above A summer herbaceous border can look spectacular, with stately hollyhocks, elegant purple verbenas and a sea of golden-yellow achillea.

left Holly berries guarantee the garden need not lack colour even in the depths of winter.

the spring garden

CREATING A
SPRING GARDEN

Spring is one of the busiest and most exciting seasons in the garden. After months of inactivity, with rain and cold temperatures, spring growth suddenly accelerates. The major new colour is lime green as the lawn puts on new growth, and the shrubs and trees explode in thousands of buds. Daffodils emerge, then tulips that can be as subtle or extrovert as you like, followed by the exotically beautiful magnolias, and rhododendrons that can be as high as a house. Getting the garden off to a smart start could not be simpler. The following pages are full of ideas that are sure to bring plenty of variety and colour into your garden.

left *Hyacinthus orientalis* 'Pink Pearl' is a spring favourite for its scent and colour. The pairing with the two-tone blue and white pansy, *Viola* 'Universal Marina', is highly effective.

THE BEST WAY TO PLAN A SPRING GARDEN, and see just what can be achieved, is to visit some beautiful public gardens and be inspired by them. Your own designs can easily be scaled down and modified. Don't just plan a spring garden around a handful of daffodils; be sure to include some sensational shapes and colours and you will have a sensory extravaganza.

large-scale mixed planting

With planning, you can create superb floral displays. If you have a spare patch of garden, or a long stretch of path, try creating a fantastic show of spring colour. Plant a row of lime trees down the centre, add decorative large pots and urns, and then begin underplanting the limes with hundreds of bulbs and perennials in a bright jamboree of red, white, blue and yellow.

right *Muscari armeniacum* will flower for many weeks from early to mid-spring. It combines well with tulips and violas.

above right *Tulipa* 'Queen of Night' is a striking, tall-growing variety, excellent for cutting. It flowers in late spring.

Go for a mix of scillas and daffodils, tulips and anemones, primroses with pulmonarias, and fritillarias with euphorbias, and the effect will be absolutely spectacular. When you see something on that scale, and with that much verve, you realize just how startling a spring show of flowers can be.

Once the main spring show has been planned, it is easy to work back to the late winter and early spring plants, and forward to the late spring and early summer flowers. There are scores of late winter performers, and the best include the tiny *Cyclamen persicum* and *Iris danfordiae*, and shrubs like *Camellia* 'Inspiration' that will flower in late winter if it is warm.

The many late spring flowers provide a good link to the start of summer. There is a much larger choice

of these plants, and they include the showy yellow laburnums, and clematis. With the ingredients in place, all you need do is sit back and enjoy.

creating a display

It is vital, when planning a spring display, that you check the different flowering times of the bulbs and the surrounding plants. There are tulips, for example, that flower in early, mid- and late spring. If the planning gets too complicated, go for just one big show in mid-season, which offers a wonderfully extensive and showy range of tulips.

If you have never grown tulips, get hold of a specialist bulb catalogue. Tulip colours range from whites, yellows and reds (soft and brash), to subtle purples and lilacs. Others come in twin colours, including startling yellow

with red stripes like 'Flaming Parrot', and the equally startling 'Frisbee', which has white cupped flowers ringed around the rim in red.

Use plants to help focus attention on the key features, like statues, splendid large urns or imaginative, topiarized shapes. When working out where to put each colour, it is an enormous help to plan the scheme by standing at key vantage points. This immediately helps clarify which colours you need in the foreground, the middle, and far distance.

Spring is a good time to create something new, whether it is a small tub or a large, multi-coloured border. The section in the book on garden styles gives ideas on how to make the best of the springtime plants. There are also many jobs to do and the essential tasks are covered – follow this advice for a successful and well-maintained garden.

above These *Narcissus cyclamineus* 'Jetfire', with their swept-back petals, look beautiful contrasted with an underplanting of *Crocus tommasinianus* 'Ruby Giant'.

SPRING PLANTS

The key to good gardening is a design that keeps the whole scheme alive, year after year, with beauty and panache, using supplementary plants to add a wide range of features. You need tiny plants for underplanting and small spaces, large shrubs to add impact, flowers for colour and scent, and surprises like the climbing *Akebia quinata* with its brownish-purple flowers. The following plant gallery, divided into bulbs, annuals, perennials, shrubs, climbers and trees, has enough high-quality, top-grade plants to turn any garden into an excellent spring showpiece.

left *Tulipa* 'Blue Parrot' in a massed bedding display with *Aubrieta* 'Royal Red'.

bulbs

Not all the plants that are called bulbs are true bulbs; some are actually corms, tubers or rhizomes. But they are all equally easy to plant and grow. It is best to buy and plant them the moment they are available, choosing fresh, firm, healthy stock. Avoid any bulbs that have come into premature growth by putting out green shoots, or which are soft, hollow or blemished.

The planting depths for bulbs will vary, and the best guide is the size of the bulb. Dig a hole that is twice the length of the bulb when the soil is on the heavy side, and three times its length when it is lighter and more free-draining.

After flowering, leave the foliage to die down naturally. This takes about six weeks, or four with smaller bulbs like crocuses. During this time the plant stores energy for next season's display. If the bulbs' foliage is cut too soon, next season's display will be adversely affected. When the bulbs are growing in a lawn, it will mean you have to wait until they have died down before mowing the grass in that area.

below left to right
Chionodoxa luciliae, Anemone blanda and *Crocus sieberi* subsp. *sublimis* 'Tricolor'.

Anemone blanda

Commonly known as the windflower, anemones are solitary flowers, about 2.5cm (1in) or more across. They have 10 to 15 white, pale blue or dark blue, sometimes mauve and pink petals. The attractive leaves are fern-like. They associate beautifully with primroses and all early dwarf daffodils, and are excellent in garden borders, beneath a tree or in pots. They form lovely, spreading flower clumps.
Flowering height 10–15cm (4–6in)
Flowering time Late winter to early spring, over 6 to 8 weeks
Hardiness Fully hardy

Camassia leichtlinii subsp. *leichtlinii*

This camassia is also known as the Indian lily and bears tall racemes, 10–30cm (4–12in) long, of star-shaped, creamy white or blue flowers, each 5–7.5cm (2–3in) across. It associates well with *Narcissus poeticus* var. *recurvus* (pheasant's eye narcissus).
Flowering height 75cm (30in)
Flowering time Late spring to early summer
Hardiness Frost hardy

Chionodoxa luciliae

This will naturalize in borders or beneath trees. It has up to 3 star-shaped, blue flowers, 1–2cm (½ – ¾in) wide and with white centres, are borne in racemes.

Flowering height 15cm (6in)
Flowering time Early to mid-spring
Hardiness Fully hardy

Crocus sieberi subsp. sublimis 'Tricolor'

A beautiful spring plant. Each petal has three bands of colour: yellow at the centre, white, then blue-purple.

Flowering height 5–7.5cm (2–3in)
Flowering time Late winter to early spring
Hardiness Fully hardy

Cyclamen persicum

The pink, red or white flowers have darker staining towards the mouth, and the heart-shaped leaves are often patterned. Many cultivars have been bred, and there are various shades and sizes to choose from, but look for those with a sweet scent and attractively marked foliage. Among the many florist's cyclamens are the scented, miniature Miracle Series.

Flowering height 10–20cm (4–8in)
Flowering time Early winter to early spring
Hardiness Frost tender

Erythronium dens-canis

A pretty spring flower, dog's tooth violet has dainty, swept-back petals that may be white, pink or lilac, and prominent anthers. The leaves have blue and green markings. Plant in borders or among short fine grasses.

Flowering height 10–15cm (4–6in)
Flowering time Spring
Hardiness Fully hardy

Fritillaria imperialis

An impressive flower, often known as the crown imperial, it produces a stout stem topped by impressive umbels of 3 to 6 pendent bells, which may be orange, yellow or, more often, red, out of which a crown of glossy, leaf-like bracts emerges. Both the bulbs and flowers have a distinctive foxy smell.

Flowering height 70cm (28in)
Flowering time Late spring
Hardiness Fully hardy

above *Fritillaria imperialis.*

below left to right
Cyclamen persicum, Camassia leichtlinii subsp. *leichtlinii* and *Erythronium dens-canis.*

above *Hyacinthus orientalis* 'Amethyst'.

below left to right *Hyacinthus orientalis* 'Jan Bos', *H. orientalis* 'Blue Jacket' and *H. orientalis* 'Hollyhock'.

Hyacinthoides non-scripta

The English bluebell bears single blue, sometimes white, flowers in graceful racemes, which bend over at the tip. Up to 12 pendent, narrow, bell-shaped, scented flowers are borne on one side only. Ideal for naturalizing beneath orchard trees. The pretty white form is known as *H. non-scripta* 'Alba'.
Flowering height 20–40cm (8–16in)
Flowering time Spring
Hardiness Fully hardy

Hyacinthus

Commonly known as the hyacinth, this is one of the most fragrant of all spring-flowering bulbs.

H. orientalis 'Amethyst'

Racemes of up to 40 single, lilac-amethyst, waxy, tubular, bell-shaped flowers, which are richly scented and are borne on stout, leafless stems.
Flowering height 20cm (8in)
Flowering time Spring outdoors (earlier indoors)
Hardiness Fully hardy

H. orientalis 'Blue Jacket'

The scented racemes of up to 40 single, dark blue, waxy, tubular, bell-shaped flowers make a good display.
Flowering height 20cm (8in)
Flowering time Spring outdoors (earlier indoors)
Hardiness Fully hardy

H. orientalis 'Hollyhock'

The double, crimson-red, tubular, bell-shaped flowers are richly scented and are borne on stout, leafless stems. 'Hollyhock' will combine beautifully with blue polyanthus primroses or perhaps with *Tanacetum parthenium* 'Aureum' (golden feverfew).
Flowering height 20cm (8in)
Flowering time Spring outdoors (earlier indoors)
Hardiness Fully hardy

H. orientalis 'Jan Bos'

The racemes have up to 40 single, cerise-red, tubular, bell-shaped flowers, which are scented and excellent with violas or primroses.
Flowering height 20cm (8in)
Flowering time Spring outdoors (earlier indoors)
Hardiness Fully hardy

Iris

This is a large genus of winter-, spring- and summer-flowering bulbs, rhizomes and fleshy rooted perennials.

I. danfordiae

A Reticulata iris with scented, lemon-yellow flowers, 5cm (2in) across which have green markings. They can be grown in the garden or in small pots.
Flowering height 10cm (4in)
Flowering time Late winter to early spring
Hardiness Fully hardy

I. 'Purple Sensation'

The purple-blue and bronze-yellow flowers of this Dutch iris are 7.5–10cm (3–4in) across. They work well under an arch of laburnum or wisteria and make excellent cut flowers. They also look very good near a pond, or planted around a pillar or statue.

Flowering height 45cm (18in)
Flowering time Late spring to early summer
Hardiness Fully hardy

Muscari

The genus, known by the common name of grape hyacinth, embraces 30 species of bulbs from the Mediterranean to south-western Asia. The best known is *Muscari armeniacum*, whose cultivars are pretty and very useful in borders, grassland and all sizes of containers.

M. armeniacum

Dense racemes of blue flowers are borne in bunches at the top of the stem. The exquisite colouring and long flowering make up for any waywardness of the foliage. Several cultivars are available, including double, soft blue 'Blue Spike' which, at 15cm (6in), is vigorous but slightly shorter than the species.

Flowering height 20cm (8in)
Flowering time Early to mid-spring
Hardiness Fully hardy

M. botryoides 'Album'

This muscari has slender racemes of scented white flowers. It is daintier than *M. armeniacum*.

Flowering height 15–20cm (6–8in)
Flowering time Early to mid-spring
Hardiness Fully hardy

above left to right *Iris danfordiae, Hyacinthoides non-scripta* 'Alba' (English bluebell) and *Muscari botryoides* 'Album'.

below left to right *Iris* 'Purple Sensation', *Muscari armeniacum* 'Blue Spike' and *Hyacinthoides non-scripta*.

Narcissus

Often known as the daffodil, this is one of the best loved of all bulbs, and the genus includes about 50 species that grow in a variety of habitats in Europe and northern Africa.

N. 'Actaea'

The pure white flowers have a brilliant scarlet eye. This is a delightful narcissus for borders or grasslands, and is an exceptionally good naturalizer.
Flowering height 45cm (18in)
Flowering time Mid-spring
Hardiness Fully hardy

N. bulbocodium

The hoop-petticoat daffodil, as this species is known, looks different from other narcissi. Allow it to naturalize on damp grassy slopes that dry out in summer.
Flowering height 10–15cm (4–6in)
Flowering time Mid-spring
Hardiness Fully hardy

N. 'Carlton'

This is a soft yellow daffodil with a large cup, which is frilly at the mouth. An excellent naturalizer, it is a delightful daffodil for borders or grassland.
Flowering height 45cm (18in)
Flowering time Mid-spring
Hardiness Fully hardy

N. cyclamineus

The golden flower has a distinctive shape with its sharply swept-back petals and long, narrow cup.
Flowering height 15–20cm (6–8in)
Flowering time Early spring
Hardiness Fully hardy

N. 'February Gold'

This is one of the best of all the early dwarf daffodils, elegant, long in flower, sturdy, short and useful in so many different parts of the garden.
Flowering height 25cm (10in)
Flowering time Early spring
Hardiness Fully hardy

N. papyraceus

Formerly known as N. 'Paper White', this daffodil bears bunches of 5 to 10 fragrant, white flowers.
Flowering height 40cm (16in)
Flowering time Spring, or winter indoors
Hardiness Frost hardy

N. 'Pipit'

Perhaps 2 to 3 exquisite two-toned flowers, each with a white cup and lemon-yellow petals, are borne on each stem. The flowers are sweetly scented.
Flowering height 30cm (12in)
Flowering time Mid- to late spring outdoors
Hardiness Fully hardy

N. 'Rip van Winkle'

This is a good choice for growing in short grass, at the front of borders or in small containers. It has striking double yellow flowers.
Flowering height 15cm (6in)
Flowering time Early spring
Hardiness Fully hardy

N. 'Suzy'

Clusters of 1 to 4 yellow flowers with flattened orange cups are borne on each stem. It is bred from fragrant N. jonquilla and inherits its strong perfume.
Flowering height 40cm (16in)
Flowering time Mid-spring
Hardiness Fully hardy

N. 'Thalia'

One of the taller dwarf daffodils, this has wonderful white flowers, often 2 or more to a stem.
Flowering height 30cm (12in)
Flowering time Mid-spring
Hardiness Fully hardy

above *Narcissus papyraceus.*

opposite from top, left to right *Narcissus* 'Pipit', *N. cyclamineus* and *N.* 'Carlton', *N. bulbocodium*, *N.* 'Actaea' and *N.* 'February Gold', *N.* 'Rip van Winkle', *N.* 'Suzy' and *N.* 'Thalia'.

Tulipa

Tulips come in all shapes and sizes, with the smallest miniature kind growing about 10cm (4in) high, and the tallest tulip being about 60cm (2ft) high. Dig them up when they have died down, and store the bulbs in a dry airy place over summer for replanting in late autumn.

early spring tulips

Every spring garden needs some tulips. They provide fantastic flashes of colour, from soft hues to brasher, eye-catching combinations. Scores are single-coloured but hundreds have two colours.

T. 'Corona'

This hybrid is sometimes called a water-lily tulip. The long buds, often cream flushed with pink, open into stars of oval petals that expose different colour combinations. Their small size makes them ideal for the rock garden and formal beds.

Flowering height 15–20cm (6–8in)
Flowering time Early spring
Hardiness Fully hardy

T. 'Madame Lefeber'

A Fosteriana hybrid, with large, brilliant scarlet flowers. This is also known as 'Red Emperor', and is one of the best early red tulips.
Flowering height 20–40cm (8–16in)
Flowering time Early to mid-spring
Hardiness Fully hardy

T. 'Peach Blossom'

A Double Early hybrid, this short, sturdy tulip bears large rose-pink flowers. In a border, it teams well with violas and bellis daisies and it is sensational when underplanted with grape hyacinths.
Flowering height 25cm (10in)
Flowering time Early to mid-spring
Hardiness Fully hardy

below left to right
Tulipa 'Corona', *T.* 'Madame Lefeber' and *T.* 'Peach Blossom'.

mid-spring tulips

There is a huge colour range of mid-season tulips and many are beautifully marked or shaded. They are ideal for bedding and make superb cut flowers. They bloom towards the end of mid- and into late spring.

T. 'Apeldoorn'

The large scarlet flowers retain their petals for a long period of time. This tulip looks beautiful with lime-green foliage.

Flowering height 55cm (22in)
Flowering time Mid- to late spring
Hardiness Fully hardy

T. 'Apricot Parrot'

Parrot tulips look like the clowns among tulips: showy and extrovert, big and attention-grabbing, with large, lacerated, wavy, crested petals in pale apricot-yellow, with a hint of white. It makes an excellent bold cut flower, and is well worth growing in the garden if a sheltered spot can be found as it is vulnerable to wind damage.

Flowering height 45–60cm (18–24in)
Flowering time Mid- to late spring
Hardiness Fully hardy

T. 'Ballerina'

This is one of the most striking of all tulips, with its scented, orange flowers. It is excellent planted with other orange flowers or plants with bronze foliage, or in containers underplanted with deep blue pansies.

Flowering height 55cm (22in)
Flowering time Mid-spring
Hardiness Fully hardy

T. 'Plaisir'

This is vivid red outside, and vermilion inside, with lemon-yellow edges to the petals, and the foliage is beautifully mottled. Being a low grower, 'Plaisir' is suitable for pots and containers and the rock garden, as well as for formal bedding schemes.

Flowering height 15–30cm (6–12in)
Flowering time Mid-spring
Hardiness Fully hardy

T. 'Striped Bellona'

This has stunning cup-shaped, striped red and yellow flowers that will make a big impact in the garden.

Flowering height 50cm (20in)
Flowering time Mid-spring
Hardiness Fully hardy

above left to right *Tulipa* 'Apricot Parrot', *T.* 'Striped Bellona', *T.* 'Plaisir' and *T.* 'Ballerina'.

below *Tulipa* 'Apeldoorn'.

late spring tulips

Late-flowering tulips are among the most exciting, both in colour and shape.

T. 'Ballade'

These are distinctive and the tall wiry stems add to the impression of elegance. The large, open flowers are suitable for late spring bedding in sheltered areas, and also make superb cut flowers.

Flowering height 45–60cm (18–24in)
Flowering time Late spring
Hardiness Fully hardy

T. 'Blue Parrot'

A Parrot tulip, with single, large, lilac-blue flowers, and irregular crimping along the edge of the petals. It is exciting when in bud and when the flowers begin to unfurl. In borders it can be planted with pink or blue forget-me-nots, while in containers pink, lavender or violet-blue pansies are perfect.

Flowering height 60cm (24in)
Flowering time Late spring
Hardiness Fully hardy

T. 'Hamilton'

A bright golden-yellow tulip with petals that are edged with a conspicuous fringe. It is stunning in a border or makes excellent cut flowers.

Flowering height 45–60cm (18–24in)
Flowering time Late spring
Hardiness Fully hardy

T. 'Marilyn'

A bold Lily-flowered tulip, with large, open flowers like colourful stars. They are white with red stripes and a feathering of red at the base.

Flowering height 45–60cm (18–24in)
Flowering time Late spring
Hardiness Fully hardy

T. 'West Point'

This striking Lily-flowered hybrid has distinctive primrose-yellow flowers that look especially charming underplanted with blue forget-me-nots.

Flowering height 50cm (20in)
Flowering time Late spring
Hardiness Fully hardy

opposite *Tulipa* 'Marilyn'.

below left to right *Tulipa* 'Hamilton', *T.* 'Blue Parrot' and *T.* 'West Point'.

annuals

An annual is a plant that completes its life cycle within one growing season: the seed germinates, grows, flowers, sets seed and dies all within the space of a year. The seed is dormant until the return of conditions favourable to germination, usually the next spring. Biennials are similar, but take two years to complete their life cycle, usually flowering in the second year.

Annuals are unrivalled for bringing colour into the garden throughout the warmer months. They bring any border to life within a matter of weeks, and give new gardens instant style and impact. They can be used in all sizes and kinds of gardens and even in tubs, window boxes, hanging baskets and all types of containers. Many plants bring other rewards, being deliciously scented or attractive to beneficial insects, and some will provide an excellent source of cut flowers for the home.

Antirrhinum

The unique "snapping" lips of the flowers of snapdragons give them a certain appeal to children. These half-hardy annuals provide strong blocks of colour – white, yellow, orange, pink, and red (some flowers being bi-coloured) – in beds and borders. *Antirrhinum majus* Wedding Bells series and *A. majus* 'Coronette' are good late spring bedding plants. *A. majus* 'Black Prince' has deep crimson and bronze foliage.
Flowering height 45cm (18in)
Flowering time Late spring
Hardiness Half-hardy

Bellis perennis

The genus includes the pretty lawn daisies that generally appear unannounced in all gardens. This species is the parent of a number of seed strains, all producing rosettes of leaves and flowers in shades of red, pink or white. They are delightful in window boxes and are good bedding plants. 'Dresden China', a dwarf form, has small, pink, double flowers with

top A deep purple *Viola* 'Penny'.

above *Viola odorata* (sweet violet) and *Primula vulgaris*.

right *Myosotis* (forget-me-nots) are excellent spring bedding plants, and help to fill in the space around the long-stalks of *Tulipa* 'Warbler'.

quilled petals. The Habanera series cultivars bear pink, white or red, long-petalled flowerheads. Cultivars of both the Pomponette and Tasso series bear double pink, white or red flowerheads with quilled petals – the Pomponette varieties are up to 4cm (1½in) across, Tasso up to 6cm (2½in).
Flowering height 10cm (4in)
Flowering time Late spring
Hardiness Fully hardy

Lunaria annua

Honesty is an erect fast-growing, modest annual or biennial that has two seasons of interest. The pretty spring flowers are followed by distinctive, papery, oval seedheads that are excellent in dried arrangements. *Lunaria annua*, a European species, usually has purple, sometimes white, flowers in spring followed by translucent white seedheads in autumn. For white flowers only, sow seeds of *L. annua* var. *albiflora*. 'Alba Variegata' is a desirable garden form with pointed-oval, serrated, white-variegated leaves and white flowers. 'Variegata' has similar leaves but with small scented flowers in shades of purple-pink.
Flowering height 1m (3ft)
Flowering time Late spring
Hardiness Fully hardy

Myosotis sylvatica

The species has mid-blue, yellow-eyed flowers in spring and early summer and grey-green leaves. Although forget-me-nots will seed on their own freely, it is worth sowing these plants afresh every season – the named forms always have flowers of a more intense colour than their natural progeny. Indispensable for most spring bedding schemes, forget-me-nots make a classic cottage-garden combination with tulips. 'Blue Ball' is a more compact form with indigo flowers. The flowers of 'Compindi', another dwarf form, are even darker. 'Rosylva' is something of a novelty, with clear pink flowers.
Flowering height 30cm (12in)
Flowering time Spring
Hardiness Fully hardy

Viola

This endearing genus includes a delicate wild form known as heartsease, as well as rock garden plants, perennial sweet-scented violets, and the well-known pansies. Some are self-coloured, but many are attractively bi- or even tri-coloured with mask-like markings that make the flowers look like faces.
Flowering height Up to 23cm (9in)
Flowering time Late spring
Hardiness Half-hardy

above left to right *Bellis perennis* 'Tasso Rose', 'Tasso Red' and 'Tasso White', *Antihirrhinum majus* 'Black Prince', *Viola tricolor* and *Lunaria annua*.

perennials

For many, a spring garden just would not be the same without the contribution of perennials, often long-lived plants that provide interest year on year. They encompass many early-flowering plants (usually low-growing) that are delightful with spring bulbs and are good in herbaceous borders. If you have a perennial that you like, you can easily take cuttings in the summer, providing extra, free plants. Generally, a young, 10cm (4in) long, non-flowering shoot gives the best results.

Anemone

This large genus includes some excellent perennials. Their late season and tolerance make them essential plants for any garden. The flowers are carried on tall, elegant, wiry stems. They are ravishing in drifts under deciduous trees, or they can be used in borders.

A. nemorosa

Commonly known as the wood anemone, these plants bear dainty, demure, solitary white flowers, sometimes with a pink flush.

Flowering height 7.5–15cm (3–6in)
Flowering time Late spring
Hardiness Fully hardy

A. ranunculoides

The yellow wood anemone has rich yellow flowers. Though low growing, reaching 10cm (4in) high at most, it spreads well and makes a beautiful show.
Flowering height 5–10cm (2–4in)
Flowering time Mid-spring
Hardiness Fully hardy

Convallaria majalis

With flowers of instantly recognizable fragrance, lily-of-the-valley is a deservedly popular cottage-garden plant. This species spreads by means of branching underground rhizomes. The handsome leaves emerge in spring and are followed in late spring by elegant sprays of bell-shaped, fragrant white flowers. The plants can also be potted up and forced under glass for early flowers. All are toxic.
Flowering height 23cm (9in)
Flowering time Mid- to late spring
Hardiness Fully hardy

Dicentra formosa

Easy plants to grow, dicentras have ferny foliage and elegant, arching stems. They are excellent in shady rock gardens or light woodland, but they also tolerate more open conditions, combining well with cottage-garden plants, such as aquilegias, flowering around the same time in late spring. *D. formosa* var. *alba* is the desirable white form.

Flowering height 45cm (18in)
Flowering time Late spring to early summer
Hardiness Fully hardy

Erysimum

Wallflowers and tulips are a classic cottage garden combination. The plants described here are all true evergreen perennials, and although they are often short-lived, cuttings easily increase them. All are of hybrid origin.

E. 'Bowles' Mauve'

This perennial belongs in every garden. Officially it produces its four-petalled, fragrant, rich mauve flowers from late winter to early summer, but it is seldom without flowers at any time of year.

Flowering height Up to 75cm (30in)
Flowering time Mid- to late spring
Hardiness Fully hardy

Euphorbia polychroma

The true flowers of euphorbia are insignificant, but are surrounded by showy bracts (referred to as 'flowers') that continue to attract attention after the true flowers have faded. All are easy to grow, but care needs to be taken when handling them: when cut or broken, the stems exude a milky sap that can cause skin irritations, particularly in bright sunshine. Always wear a good pair of gardening gloves. *E. polychroma* is a must for the spring garden, making a mound of foliage that in late spring becomes a mass of brilliant yellow-green as the flowers open.

Flowering height 30cm (12in)
Flowering time Mid-spring to midsummer
Hardiness Fully hardy

Helleborus foetidus

Hellebores have nodding flowers and handsome, more or less evergreen leaves. All are poisonous, but handling them will not produce any problems. *H. foetidus* (stinking hellebore) makes a clump of blackish-green leaves. Strong stems carrying many bell-shaped, apple-green flowers appear from late winter to early spring. It looks good with snowdrops.

Flowering height 75cm (30in)
Flowering time Into early spring
Hardiness Fully hardy

above *Erysimum* 'Bowles Mauve'.

below left to right *Dicentra formosa, Convallaria majalis* and *Euphorbia polychroma.*

Primula

This large and complex genus, which includes the well-known primroses, contains about 400 species of perennials, some suitable for mixed plantings, others for bedding, while a few are happiest in a rock garden.

The plants that are described here do well in cool, damp atmospheres and moisture-retentive, preferably neutral soil. All have characteristic rosettes of spoon-shaped leaves from which the flowering stems arise. Another characteristic (but not of all) is 'farina', a flour-like bloom on the stems and leaves that can provoke an allergic reaction.

Shorter growing primulas are delightful with dwarf spring bulbs and are good in window boxes. Primroses and polyanthus are archetypal cottage-garden plants, while moisture-lovers are effective near water, preferably the running water of a stream. Primroses are among the few plants that combine happily with rhododendrons, as well as being good companions for the smaller hostas. So-called Candelabra types are distinctive and graceful plants, with flowers carried in whorls up the stems, and need rich, moist soil.

below left to right *Primula japonica, P. japonica* 'Miller's Crimson' and *P. vulgaris.*

opposite *Primula beesiana.*

P. beesiana

This Candelabra primula, which is deciduous or semi-evergreen, produces whorls of cerise-pink flowers in tiers on long, sturdy stems.
Flowering height 60cm (2ft)
Flowering time Late spring to early summer
Hardiness Fully hardy

P. japonica

In moist, shady places in Japan, this pretty, deciduous primula thrives and produces red-purple to white Candelabra-type flowers.
Flowering height 45cm (18in)
Flowering time Mid-spring
Hardiness Fully hardy

P. veris

The evergreen or semi-evergreen yellow-flowered cowslip is a familiar sight in damp meadows. It can be established in grass, as long as the ground is moist.
Flowering height 25cm (10in)
Flowering time Late spring
Hardiness Fully hardy

shrubs

Shrubs encompass a wide range, from tree-like plants (which can substitute for trees in small gardens) to more diminutive ones that can be used in rock gardens or as ground cover. Most are grown for their often-spectacular flowers, but others have less obvious attractions – showy berries or good leaf colour or an appealing habit. Judiciously chosen, shrubs give an air of permanence to any planting.

Camellia

This is a large genus, containing about 250 species of superb evergreen shrubs and small trees, made larger by the number of hybrids. Unfortunately for many gardens they must have acid soil, but, they thrive in containers where you can provide suitable conditions. Use camellias as specimens in large tubs or barrels in courtyards or patios, or in shrub borders. All camellias have lustrous green leaves, making them splendid backdrops to other plants when they have finished flowering.

below left to right
Camellia 'Elizabeth Hawkins', *Ceanothus* 'Dark Star' and *Camellia* 'Jury's Yellow'.

C. 'Elizabeth Hawkins'

A cultivar of *C. japonica*. It has anemone-form, bright pinkish-red flowers.
Height 2m (6ft)
Flowering time Mid-spring
Hardiness Fully hardy

C. 'Inspiration'

A reliable, upright plant (verging on a small tree) that has semi-double, deep pink flowers. This is good when trained as a wall shrub.
Height 4m (13ft)
Flowering time Midwinter to late spring
Hardiness Fully hardy

C. 'Jury's Yellow'

One of the *C. x williamsii* hybrids. The slow-growing 'Jury's Yellow' has anemone- to peony-like flowers, with creamy-white outer petals and creamy-yellow inner ones. This is the nearest to a yellow camellia.
Height 2.5m (8ft)
Flowering time Mid- to late spring
Hardiness Fully hardy

Ceanothus

The Californian lilac is highly prized for its show of true blue, deliciously scented flowers. There are deciduous and evergreen species, the evergreens being slightly more tender. In cold areas all are best grown in the shelter of a sunny wall, but in warmer climates they make truly spectacular specimens. The pink- and white-flowered types are of interest but less popular.

C. 'Dark Star'

Dark purplish-blue flowers are carried in spring on this arching evergreen.
Height 2m (6ft)
Flowering time Late spring
Hardiness Half-hardy

C. 'Delight'

This evergreen variety, which has clusters of rich blue flowers, makes a good wall shrub.
Height 3m (10ft)
Flowering time Late spring
Hardiness Half-hardy

Choisya ternata

Mexican orange blossom is a handsome evergreen with glossy green leaves and a neat, rounded habit. It flowers mostly in spring with, often, a second flush in late summer or autumn. The leaves are highly aromatic. Choisyas tolerate some shade and are good growing against a wall.
Height 2.4m (8ft)
Flowering time Spring
Hardiness Fully hardy

Daphne

Evergreen, semi-evergreen or deciduous, these shrubs bear flowers with an exquisite fragrance. Some are rock garden plants, but most thrive in borders. Winter-flowering types are best sited near a door where their fragrance can be appreciated to the full, without the need to go too far outdoors. *D. tangutica* is a small, evergreen species with fragrant white flowers comes from China.
Height 1m (3ft)
Flowering time Late spring
Hardiness Fully hardy

above left to right
Daphne tangutica, Camellia 'Inspiration' and *Choisya ternata.*

below *Ceanothus* 'Delight'.

Pieris

These elegant evergreen woodland shrubs bear racemes of lily-of-the-valley-like flowers in spring.

P. 'Forest Flame'

The flush of leafy growth in spring is brilliant red.
Height 2.2m (7ft)
Flowering time Mid- to late spring
Hardiness Borderline hardy

P. japonica

Lily-of-the-valley bush has glossy green leaves and cascading sprays of white flowers in spring. Good forms include 'Pink Delight', 'Valley Rose' and the prolific 'Valley Valentine'.
Height 3m (10ft)
Flowering time Late winter to spring
Hardiness Fully hardy

Rhododendron

This large genus includes plants that range from huge, tree-like shrubs to diminutive specimens for a rock garden or alpine trough. All need acid soil.

R. 'Bruce Brechtbill'

This has a dense habit and pale pink flowers.
Height 2m (6ft)
Flowering time Late spring to early summer
Hardiness Fully hardy

R. 'Cary Ann'

A compact shrub with coral pink flowers that is good for small gardens.
Height 1.5m (5ft)
Flowering time Late spring to early summer
Hardiness Fully hardy

R. 'Chanticleer'

A spectacular plant that produces a rich display of maroon-purple flowers.
Height 1.5m (5ft)
Flowering time Late spring to early summer
Hardiness Fully hardy

R. 'Grace Seabrook'

A robust and vigorous form bearing conical trusses of deep pink, often reddish flowers.
Height 2m (6ft)
Flowering time Early to mid-spring
Hardiness Fully hardy

Viburnum carlesii

This deciduous species from Japan and Korea is almost unmatched for the scent of its white spring flowers, pink in bud and carried in rounded clusters. 'Diana' has purplish-pink flowers that fade to white.
Height 1.5m (5ft)
Flowering time Spring
Hardiness Fully hardy

opposite, clockwise from top left *Rhododendron 'Bruce Brechtbill', Pieris 'Forest Flame', Rhododendron 'Cary Ann' and Pieris japonica.*

above left to right *Rhododendron 'Chanticleer', Viburnum carlesii 'Diana' and Rhododendron 'Grace Seabrook'.*

climbers

These are among the most dramatic and rewarding garden plants, lifting your eyes skywards as they reach towards the sun. They are ideal for beautifying walls, fences and ugly outbuildings, and can also be draped over pergolas to provide welcome shade, or used to carpet banks. Some have spectacular flowers that emerge in spring and can be deliciously scented. Others are grown for their leaves, while the evergreens provide year-round interest.

Clematis

There is a clematis for virtually every season of the year. All the following, group 1, flower during the spring on the previous year's growth. Prune the bushes after flowering.

C. armandii

This species, one of the few evergreen clematis, has long, leathery, dark green leaves and clusters of scented, white flowers in spring. A vigorous plant, it is best trained against a warm wall in cold areas. 'Apple Blossom' is pale pink.
Height 3m (10ft)
Flowering time Early spring
Hardiness Borderline hardy

below left to right *Wisteria sinensis, Clematis macropetala* with buds of *C. montana, C. montana* 'Continuity' and *Wisteria floribunda.*

C. cirrhosa

This is usually the first clematis to flower and typically it begins to bloom in midwinter, but some flowers can be produced as early as autumn. These are bell-shaped, with a papery texture, and are creamy-white in colour, sometimes speckled with brownish-red inside.
Height 3m (10ft)
Flowering time Late winter to early spring
Hardiness Borderline hardy

C. macropetala

The bell-shaped flowers of this species, which appear in mid- to late spring, have only four petals, but appear to be double because some of the stamens are petal-like. They are blue or violet-blue. 'Blue Bird' has semi-double, clear blue flowers. The charming 'White Moth' (syn. *C. alpina* 'White Moth') has pure white flowers.
Height 3m (10ft)
Flowering time Spring to early summer
Hardiness Fully hardy

C. montana

The most vigorous of the early clematis, this is the last to flower. Species include 'Continuity', with creamy-white, pink-tinged flowers; 'Elizabeth', which has pale pink, richly scented flowers; and the vigorous *C. montana* f. *grandiflora*, with white flowers.

Height 6m (20ft)
Flowering time Late spring and early summer
Hardiness Fully hardy

Wisteria

Possibly the most desirable of all flowering climbers, wisterias bear dramatic racemes of scented pea flowers from late spring to early summer. Old specimens trained against house walls are breath-taking, as are those trained to embrace arching bridges over water. They are also spectacular growing over arches, pergolas or – in a less formal garden – allowed to ramp into sturdy host trees. When buying wisterias, look for named varieties grafted on to vigorous rootstocks, expensive though these are.

W. floribunda

The Japanese wisterias are slightly shorter than the Chinese kind, but have equally long racemes of scented flowers. In a warm spell they will appear in late spring, otherwise slightly later. Good forms include 'Multijuga' whose racemes of light blue flowers can reach 1m (3ft) long. 'Alba' has white flowers. 'Violacea Plena' has double flowers verging on purple.
Height 9m (30ft)
Flowering time Late spring and early summer
Hardiness Fully hardy

W. sinensis

The Chinese wisterias tend to be more vigorous than the Japanese kind. The species has faintly-scented, violet-blue flowers that appear in 20–30cm (8–12in) long racemes before the leaves. Two other good forms worth growing are the white-flowering 'Alba', and 'Caroline' with slightly larger, rich blue-purple flowers. 'Prolific' lives up to its name, and produces a superb show of flowers that will not let you down.
Height 15m (50ft)
Flowering time Late spring and early summer
Hardiness Fully hardy

above *C. montana* 'Elizabeth'

below A beautiful well-established wisteria in full bloom covering the front of a house.

trees

A tree completes a garden. Whether it is grown for its flowers, fruits, foliage or overall appearance, a tree adds dignity and style to any garden. From oaks to the more manageable Japanese maples, there is a tree for every type of garden whether you have rolling acres or a suburban plot. Even if you have only a courtyard, balcony or roof garden, there are trees suitable for containers. Careful selection is necessary, as a tree often outlives the gardener.

Acacia dealbata

Mimosa or silver wattle is a pretty evergreen Australian and Tasmanian species with silver-grey, fern-like leaves and masses of fragrant, fluffy yellow flowers from late winter to early spring. It is suitable for training against a sunny, warm sheltered wall.
Height 15m (50ft)
Flowering time Early spring
Hardiness Half-hardy

Cercis siliquastrum

The unusual Judas tree, native to south-eastern Europe and south-western Asia, is quick-growing and produces dark pink flowers on the bare wood in spring. The kidney-shaped, blue-green leaves turn yellow in autumn. The tree can be trained against a wall. The shrubby form *C. siliquastrum* f. *albida* has white flowers and pale green leaves.
Height 10m (33ft)
Flowering time Mid-spring
Hardiness Fully hardy

below left A smart combination with a magnolia tree under-planted with grape hyacinths.

below right *Acacia dealbata*.

Magnolia

Sumptuous and stately, magnolias are among the most handsome of garden trees, as well as being among the hardiest. Drawbacks of some of the species are their enormous size, slowness of growth and reluctance to flower until some 20 or more years after planting. Fortunately, most of the modern selections are free from these vices. The deciduous spring-flowerers make excellent features.

M. campbellii

The large, cup-and-saucer-shaped flowers, to 30cm (12in) across, are either white or pink.
Height 15m (50ft)
Flowering time Late winter to early spring
Hardiness Fully hardy

M. 'Pickard's Schmetterling'

A spreading tree, this bears goblet-shaped, rich pinkish-purple flowers. The flowers open as the leaves emerge.
Height 10m (33ft)
Flowering time Mid-spring
Hardiness Fully hardy

M. stellata

Star magnolia is a slow-growing, deciduous species. It is indispensable in a spring garden with masses of beautiful, spidery white flowers. It requires a sheltered spot.
Height 1.2m (4ft)
Flowering time Mid-spring
Hardiness Fully hardy

Malus 'John Downie'

As well as a plethora of fruit-bearing trees, this genus includes a number of trees of ornamental value that suit cottage-style gardens. M. 'John Downie' is one of the finest crab apples, and the best for making jelly. The cup-shaped, white flowers are followed by quantities of egg-shaped, orange and red fruits.
Height 6m (20ft)
Flowering time Late spring
Hardiness Fully hardy

Prunus 'Hillieri'

There are a huge number of ornamental cherry trees. A cherry orchard is a spectacular sight when in flower, and an ornamental cherry should be among the first choices for a flowering specimen. P. 'Hillieri' is a spreading tree with clusters of soft pink flowers. P. x cistena has pink flowers with purple centres.
Height 10m (33ft)
Flowering time Mid-spring
Hardiness Fully hardy

Sorbus aria 'Lutescens'

This form of whitebeam is more compact than the species, and so is better suited to medium gardens. The leaves are covered in creamy-white hairs and are brilliant as they emerge in the spring. The heads of white flowers that appear in late spring are followed by red berries. Another good choice is S. aria 'Majestica'.
Height 10m (33ft)
Flowering time Late spring
Hardiness Fully hardy

above left to right
Magnolia campbellii, Sorbus aria 'Lutescens', *Prunus* x *cistena* and *Magnolia* 'Pickard's Schmetterling'.

below *Prunus* x *subhirtella*.

SPRING DISPLAYS

There are so many different styles of gardening, whether your taste is for a Mediterranean look, a rampant, half-wild cottage garden, or a highly formal design with neat, ordered beds. Whatever form of garden you choose, you can highlight spring plants in a host of exciting ways in beds, borders, or around a pond or water feature. There are also all kinds of unusual pots and tubs for patios and window boxes to make great displays.

left This mixed spring border includes bold groups of daffodils, red and yellow tulips and wallflowers edged with blue primroses.

planting out

Bulbs and spring-flowering plants such as primroses can be planted in many ways, for example, in beds and borders, under trees and in lawns.

naturalization

Most gardens have a patch of lawn, even if they are not very big, providing a chance to plant bulbs in what is called the 'natural way'. This means, quite simply, letting the bulbs grow through the grass, and this is especially effective around the base of deciduous trees. The canopy of leaves will not yet have emerged, which means that sunlight and moisture will still be able to reach the ground beneath the crown. The area can then be filled with just one sort of bulb such as *Narcissus* 'February Gold' or a massed planting of, say, scillas or chionodoxas. Once planted, you can leave them to take care of themselves for years on end, and the effect, without fail, works every time. They will multiply freely, only needing occasional dividing if they become too congested.

When planting the bulbs, make sure you allow plenty of space for them to spread. The best way to

right *Crocus vernus* naturalized in grass.

right *Narcissus* 'February Gold' is one of the best of the early dwarf daffodils. Lustrous in colour, it is early to flower, sturdy and long lasting. Planted en masse, it creates a generous flash of yellow beneath an old cherry tree.

far right A bank of *Scilla bithynica* looks marvellous in the dappled light beneath a broad deciduous tree.

achieve a natural, non-contrived look is to take a handful of bulbs and freely scatter them on the ground, then plant them where they fall. To plant in a lawn, you can either dig individual holes for each bulb or pull back a strip of lawn for several bulbs. The former involves using a trowel, or a bulb planter that pulls out a plug of earth. Fork up and loosen the base of the hole, pop in the bulb and cover. When removing a strip of lawn, slice through the ground with a spade on three sides of a square, and then roll it back. In both cases it is absolutely vital that you use vigorous, quick spreading bulbs such as *Crocus tommasinianus* that can compete with the tough grass. If the grass is quite fine, then you should have no problems using less vigorous bulbs. You can cheat and get a longer show of naturalized flowers by planting several bulbs at a slightly deeper depth than normal.

colourful ideas

Use fresh yellow in spring, but do not overdo it. There is a wide range of other colours. For example, scented hyacinths come in white, blue, pink and crimson, primroses in just about every shade you can think of, and daffodils in white, pink, orange and marmalade. Keep schemes lively and varied.

It is also vital that the colour schemes, no matter how beautiful, combine well with the adjoining arrangement. A sensational foreground show of gentle pinks will immediately lose its impact if planted under a cherry tree with a great aerial display of pink blossom. Choosing the right colour means being able to set it off against colours that will highlight your planting scheme and not diminish it.

For strength and warmth of colour, plant the brighter, richer-coloured tulips and grape hyacinths among vibrant red, orange or blue polyanthus primroses or amid the blues and purples of violas and pansies. Plan the borders in autumn and reap the rewards in spring. The results will be well worth the care taken over planning.

above *Tulipa* 'Orange Nassau' is a vibrant orange-red and associates well with red polyanthus. You could also include *Tanacetum parthenium* 'Aureum' (golden feverfew) or bright green herbaceous plants.

left Try planting two kinds of bulbs together. Here *Scilla sibirica* has been planted between 'Pink Pearl' hyacinths.

below Tulips and blue camassias are used lavishly in this border of shrubs and herbaceous plants.

right Daffodils and anemones contrast wonderfully together.

opposite Bright spring flowering borders with large groups of *Tulipa* 'Christmas Marvel'.

beds and borders

If your garden does not hit a full colourful stride until early summer, it needs a large injection of spring-flowering performers. This means either spring bedding (one-season plants subsequently removed to make way for summer annuals, for example), or more permanent plants. The big problem, when digging planting holes, is remembering exactly where other plants are deep down in the ground. The last thing you want when digging a hole is to hear a sound like a speared potato as your fork plunges into an allium bulb.

One good way round the problem is to plant bulbs that enjoy light shade under and around shrubs, where nothing else is growing. Then, when the bulbs die down in early summer, the shrubs take over. You can mark other planting positions the previous summer, when you can see what is growing where, by placing bricks or stones where you want the planting holes. It might look odd for a while, but it is only for a few months. This also helps clarify exactly how many spring plants you have room for. Try to avoid sporadic, isolated shows of colour, and aim for lively spring combinations with at least two or three different kinds of plants with plenty of style. One classic combination is yellow tulips with blue forget-me-nots.

containers

There is one excellent reason for growing spring plants in containers. No matter how bad the weather, with late spring frosts and freezing conditions, you can keep the containers in the greenhouse, in relative warmth, ready for putting out when conditions improve. Do make sure that you gently acclimatize them to outside conditions first, though.

Growing plants in containers also means that you can keep some plants indoors, in the warmth, forcing an early spring show instead of the one that would normally occur, say, at the end of the season. And the third and final benefit of growing spring plants or bulbs in containers is that you can highlight and position them exactly where you like, instead of having their positions dictated by the garden layout.

hanging baskets

You certainly get the biggest and showiest displays in the summer, but that does not mean that you cannot create some excellent spring displays.

Begin by buying a large hanging basket, into which you can pack plenty of plants. Sit the basket firmly on a large pot or bucket, and then line the inside of the bottom half of the basket with one of the many types of liners available, such as sphagnum moss, and half fill with potting compost (soil mix). Then carefully insert the roots of the chosen plants from the outside, in. When the bottom half has been planted, firm in the root balls with more compost, and then add sphagnum around the top inner half of the basket. Continue planting up in this way.

Excellent plants include trailing, small-leaved, variegated ivies to hang down, bright pansies around the sides, hyacinths and small, highly-scented narcissi

left Blue *Muscari* (grape hyacinth) and red tulips blend beautifully together.

like Jonquils (especially when the hanging baskets are at head height so that you can smell them), tulips and wallflowers. For a smart vertical focal point, try a young thin conifer that can later be planted out in the garden. When hanging up the basket remember that after it has been watered it will be very heavy, and that strong 'fixings' are required to make sure it does not crash down.

right This gorgeous hanging basket is a stylish mixture of *Viola* 'Bowles Black', *V.* 'Johnny Jump Up' and *V.* x *wittrockiana* with Double Early tulips and *Muscari armeniacum* (grape hyacinth).

below *Bellis perennis* 'Tasso Red' and 'Tasso Rose', *Primula veris,* and violas give visual interest to this unusual edible hanging basket full of parsley, rosemary, eau-de-cologne mint, marjoram and golden lemon balm.

window boxes

You cannot beat a bright show of colours right outside your window. Unlike hanging baskets, which usually look better with an array of plants, boxes can be elegant and stylish with just one kind of plant. That can be a row of hyacinths, so that their scent can waft indoors on warm days when the window is open, or the smaller, elegant narcissi like *N. cyclamineus* 'Jack Snipe', with white petals and a yellow centre. The effect can be enormously improved by placing shapely pebbles and stones on the soil surface. You can even go one better by painting the window box a contrasting colour, for example rich blue or slate grey, or for something slightly livelier try dark red with thin yellow, curving wispy lines.

above left A small metal window box planted with narcissi is perfect for a kitchen windowsill or for the conservatory.

above right Window boxes in subdued, natural wood are the perfect foil for a vibrant display of colourful spring flowers.

right An eye-catching window box with *Narcissus* 'Hawera', *Viola* 'Sunbeam' and *V.* 'White Perfection' set off by the silver-grey foliage of *Senecio cineraria*.

tubs, pots and scent

If you have a spare patch of patio or terrace, it is well worth patterning it with a smart range of tubs and pots so that they are almost as eye-catching as the plants. Aim for a variety of styles from large, impressive urns down to smaller, old-fashioned pots for crocuses.

The bigger pots need strong, dominant plants. They might include tender plants that were moved under cover over winter, like the fantastically dramatic *Agave americana* with its long, stiff, fleshy pointed leaves that can grow 2m (6ft) long. At this time of year it needs a warm, sheltered spot, and a quick dash into the conservatory if there is a sudden frost.

Camellias are far less demanding, especially the smaller hardy ones like the beautiful *C.* 'Nicky Crisp'. It flowers from early to mid-spring, has pink flowers, and will not exceed 1.5m (5ft).

For one of the strongest scents in the spring garden you need *Daphne odora* 'Aureomarginata'. The pale pink flowers open in early spring. You will get the most from this slow-growing shrub, which will reach about 1.2m (4ft) high, by placing it in a sunny, windless corner.

above left *Tulipa* 'Blue Heron' and orange wallflowers make a vibrant combination. The gentle scent from the wallflowers is an added bonus.

above *Hippeastrum* 'Red Velvet' gives a reliable spring show of colour.

above left A spring triumph of glorious soft pink tulips and early-flowering pansies in shades of blue.

above centre Tulips planted with forget-me-nots are a classic combination.

above right A pretty container full of *Viola odorata*, *Primula vulgaris* and golden feverfew plants.

right Dwarf irises, crocuses and primroses brighten up a warm day in early spring.

ceramic pots

Ceramic or clay pots really stand out in the spring garden before the summer flowers start hogging the limelight. A huge array of decorative ceramic pots are available with ornamental features, including Italian and Greek style, and they need a prominent position. They also need clever, imaginative planting that will not let them down.

Some of the most intriguing spring plants include the fritillarias. *Fritillaria imperialis* (crown imperial) grow about 1.5m (5ft) high, and need big bold pots. The stems have plenty of leaves lower down, with a bare stretch above, and right at the top stunning, downward-pointing yellow, orange or red flowers.

Far smaller, but almost as startling, are the 50cm (20in) high red and yellow tulips, *Tulipa acuminata*. They need 45cm (18in) wide pots, and a light background that will show off their spidery thin petals, 10cm (4in) long, yellow at the base and bright red towards the tip. They add an exotic touch. But even without such plants, most displays look good in ceramic. It adds immediate style.

other containers

It is all too easy to limit oneself when buying pots, by sticking to the tried and tested such as clay and plastic. You can use all kinds of containers such as old wooden barrels, provided they have drainage holes in the bottom. It does not even matter if your containers are flimsy, like old boots and shoes, they may only last one season, but they will make an eye-catching display.

Look around architectural salvage yards and rummage sales for fun, unusual containers. Lead or other metal ones often have patterns on the outside, and if you build up a special collection the patterns could be highlighted and arranged up a flight of steps.

Given a lightly shaded position, they look marvellous when planted with *Polygonatum* x *hybridum* (common Solomon's seal). The stems arch up and out, with dangling white flowers. You could even stand an old dresser, given a lick of paint, firmly fixed in position outside against a wall, putting a collection of unusual pots on the shelves. You can then line up old rubber boots filled with compost and daffodils, in front.

above left The delicate heads of *Primula veris* look charming alongside the pretty blue *Viola* 'Penny', planted up together in a rustic basket that would be ideal in a cottage garden.

above right The teapot is planted with violas and *Narcissus* 'Hawera', which is a neat little daffodil with a multitude of dainty lemon-yellow flowers.

right *Convallaria majalis* (lily-of-the-valley) in a metal tub from an architectural salvage yard.

spring styles

It does not matter what kind of garden style you have, whether it is smart and modern, stark and minimalist or wonderfully old-fashioned, there is always room for a strong display of spring plants. The secret is choosing the most suitable plants for your preferred style, and then finding the right position. The former is quite easy, but the latter can be incredibly tricky. Many gardeners find themselves moving plants two or three times before they are in the right position. Thereafter they should quickly flourish.

the formal style

Gardens in formal style have strong, clearly defined, regular shapes, and the plants have clearly fixed positions. Chaotic jungles they are not. When planting out bulbs like tulips, for example, aim for large, solid displays with equal spacing between each bulb. Impressive order is the keynote.

above right Subtle and cool interplanting with the lovely *Tulipa* 'Spring Green' and white bellis daisies.

right A mixed spring border includes red and yellow *Tulipa* 'Striped Bellona'.

far right Spring-flowering bedding plants such as forget-me-nots, bellis and winter-flowering pansies have been used extensively in this garden to fill in between the bulbs. These plants also help to extend the period of colour, as they bloom for a long period.

left Spring in a cottage garden bed with an abundant planting of primulas, forget-me-nots, columbines and bluebells.

below A camellia planted with *Viburnum tinus* and *Elaeagnus* makes an effective backdrop to spring-flowering perennials.

romantic ramblers

Cottage gardens have a loose, free-flowing design, with hazy boundaries between the different areas. The plants are encouraged to self-seed, ramble, and climb like clematis. While tall plants generally go to the back, and the small to the front, the rule need not always be followed.

It adds enormous and quirky fun to have the likes of three *Fritillaria imperialis* (crown imperial) shooting up beside a path, or even the back door, the flowers grow on stems that are 1.5m (5ft) high. For a low-down effect there is *Fritillaria meleagris* (snake's head fritillary), 30cm (12in) high, that will make a mosaic of pinkish-purple bells, provided the soil never dries out. Or try bulbous Juno irises that need dry, well-drained ground. The easiest to grow are the lilac *I. cycloglossa* and white to lemon-yellow *I. bucharica*. Reliable Bearded irises add a lovely floppy show of petals, and for a weird and wonderful effect go for *Arisaema griffithii*, which starts poking out of the ground in the spring like a snake. For a moist, shady site there is *Erythronium dens-canis* (dog's tooth violet) with its delicate, spiky petals. A yellow forsythia sets off the whole scene.

bold designs

Contemporary gardens make good use of modern structures, gadgets and clean, simple paving. They use painted decking, outdoor lighting, architectural plants, jets of water rather than traditional fountains, and can look like an upbeat, outdoor room. Plants can either be used to soften or accentuate the look.

Softening spring plants include blue scillas, *Anemone blanda* with starry blue, white or pink flowers, and deep blue *Chionodoxa sardensis*, with plenty of white snowdrops (*Galanthus nivalis*). Spanish bluebells (*Hyacinthoides hispanica*) give a better show than the English kind. And if you want just one or two quite beautiful flowering shrubs to set off the hard landscaping, *Rosa mutabilis* is one of the first roses to flower in spring, in a warm, sheltered site, and ends with flourishes in the autumn. The buds are flame red, with light pink flowers that darken with age.

right A strikingly unusual water feature, surrounded by a glorious mid- to late spring border of fluffy spikes of *Smilacina racemosa* (false spikenard).

below A deep blue wooden centrepiece filled with grasses is the focus of this modern patio area. Bright marigolds in the borders add colour and contrast in late spring.

sunny styles

Drought-tolerant plants are the key plants for a Mediterranean look, with pots, strong scent and bright colours. A vertical rosemary can be pruned to add shapeliness – try 'Miss Jessopp's Upright', or the upright 'Tuscan Blue'. With its dark blue spring flowers, it will catch the eye, especially when underplanted with small, bright red species tulips like *Tulipa linifolia*. Blue aubrieta on white walls also gives a terrific, early season contrast.

flamboyant planting

Decorative leaves, rich colours, interesting shapes and tender plants make up the exotic garden. Top of any shopping list is a cherry tree for its sensational spring blossom and a *Gunnera manicata* (given a large patch of damp soil) for its new spring growth of sharply-toothed leaves that grow like satellite dishes to 2.5m (8ft) high. You also need a *Magnolia stellata* (star magnolia) with its pretty white flowers. Add a bamboo and *Iris reticulata*, and the picture is complete.

above left Lush, richly colourful rhododendrons.

above A collection of pots with bright grape hyacinths create a Mediterranean feel.

water gardens

right Moisture-loving plants, such as ferns and candelabra primulas, create an almost tropical atmosphere around this informal pool.

below A naturalistic waterfall nestling within a rock garden contrasts with the smooth, semicircular slate paving and the fresh green foliage and yellow spring flowers.

Ponds slowly revive in the spring as the water starts to warm up. For a wide range of wildlife do not add fish because they will eat anything small that moves, especially tadpoles. With luck newts will move in. The young frogs and newts like a still, shallow, sheltered patch of water where they can safely mature, usually amongst the emerging shoots of irises. There are two kinds of irises for wet ground, those that like bog gardens (*Iris ensata* and *I. sibirica*) and those for shallow water (*I. laevigata*, *I. pseudacorus* and *I. versicolor*). All are excellent.

Pond water tends to be on the green side for a few weeks, until the oxygenating plants come to life.

A plant that looks good and helps keep the water clear is *Stratiotes aloides* (water soldier). It looks like the leaves on a pineapple. The spring-flowering *Hottonia palustris* (water violet) is also very effective. Both grow in deep water. For more spring flowers, try planting the yellow *Caltha palustris* (kingcup) and *Myosotis scorpioides* (water forget-me-not). The last two like the shallow water around the edge of a pond.

above A sheltering rustic woven fence and a wood-decked seating area add a country feel to this densely planted pond surrounded by primroses, irises and soft spring colours.

right Bold blue irises soften the harsh lines of the decorative metal grille covering this pool. The grille serves as a safety feature and keeps feeding herons away from the fish.

SPRING TASKS

Spring is one of the most enjoyable times in the garden. It means preparing the soil in the borders and vegetable garden, sowing seeds of annuals, herbs, fruit and vegetables, and most important of all, making sure that all the new emerging seedlings are not slaughtered by hungry pigeons and hordes of slugs and snails. Get everything right now, and you will have great flowering displays in just a few weeks.

left The exquisite lily-flowered *Tulipa* 'West Point' vies for attention with red and yellow polyanthus, all bordered with dark blue forget-me-not, *Mysotis sylvatica* 'Music'.

above Traditionally, perennials are bought bare-rooted, having been grown in the ground and dug up when needed. Bare-rooted plants should be bought only between late autumn and early spring.

right Buying annuals in strips is a popular method of obtaining large numbers of plants at low cost. Young plants have plenty of room to develop a good root system.

early spring

In cold regions the weather can still be icy in early spring, but in mild climates you can make a start on many outdoor jobs. If sowing or planting outdoors, bear in mind that soil temperature as well as air temperature is important. Few seeds will germinate if the soil temperature is below 7°C (45°F), so use a soil thermometer to check before you sow.

kitchen gardens

Warm soil, by day and night, is particularly important when sowing tender herbs like basil. Instead of sowing all your seed now and seeing only a few plants emerge, it is better to wait until the end of spring or early summer when germination rates will be higher.

If you have cloches then use them like blankets to warm up the soil before sowing vegetables like lettuce. Otherwise, you can start sowing lettuces in small pots or buckets indoors. This gets the plants off to a racing start. Gradually harden them off, standing them outside in a sheltered place or in a cold frame, until they can be planted out. The added benefit is that being larger they are less likely to be shredded by the early morning birds. Tasty new crops should be covered by nets to keep pigeons away, and beer traps

above When planting new herbaceous plants, make sure the ground is weed-free and start at the rear of the border.

the flower garden

- ❖ Finish planting bare-root trees and shrubs
- ❖ Plant container-grown shrubs
- ❖ Plant herbaceous plants
- ❖ Sow hardy annuals, like sweet peas
- ❖ Feed and mulch beds and borders
- ❖ Plant gladioli and other summer bulbs
- ❖ Start mowing the lawn, but cut high initially; reduce the height of the blades thereafter
- ❖ Sow a new lawn or lay a lawn from turf
- ❖ Recut or neaten edges of the lawn
- ❖ Buy seeds and bulbs if not already done so
- ❖ Prune shrubs, if necessary
- ❖ Prune roses always making sure that you cut directly above a shoot
- ❖ Tidy up the rock garden, and apply fresh stone chippings where necessary
- ❖ Clean out the pond, and make sure that there are no rotting leaves at the bottom
- ❖ Add scatterings of pelleted poultry manure on flower beds

above Cut out any diseased or damaged wood back to sound wood, just above a strong bud.

will reduce the slug numbers. Place the traps away from the new crops and not amongst them, or the slugs will reach the crops before drowning.

beds and borders

One of the biggest bugbears of gardening is the amount of time spent watering over summer. The best way to avoid this is to wait until after a few days of heavy spring rain, when the soil is deeply saturated, and then spread a thick layer of mulch such as mushroom compost over the soil. This locks in the moisture now, and after subsequent waterings. It also keeps down weeds and helps condition the soil.

cutting lawns

The best way to keep a healthy green lawn is to give it a first light cut in the spring. Thereafter give it a medium cut, or the longest possible cut for your needs, such as children's games. The longer the grass the longer the roots, and this means it will stay lusher and greener for longer during dry spells. Lawns that are cut very short have short roots that cannot go deep down for moisture during long dry spells, and they are the first to go brown.

the greenhouse and conservatory

❖ Take chrysanthemum cuttings
❖ Start off begonia and gloxinia tubers
❖ Take pelargonium and fuchsia cuttings
❖ Take dahlia cuttings
❖ Sow seeds of bedding plants and pot plants
❖ Prick out or pot up seedlings sown earlier
❖ Increase ventilation on warm days
❖ Check plants for signs of pests and diseases, which often begin to multiply rapidly as the temperature rises
❖ Container-grown fuchsias need cutting back now and repotting
❖ Untie climbers so that you can repaint or clean the backing surface
❖ Buy new pots, and paint old ones in pastel and hothouse colours
❖ Thoroughly clean out the greenhouse, checking old pots for slugs and snails
❖ Sharpen secateurs

above Seedlings are almost always pricked out individually, but lobelia seedlings are so tiny that they should be pricked out in groups of five or six at a time.

below Plant an area of bedding before positioning the bulbs between the plants.

mid-spring

above Plant up containers for summer displays.

This is when the garden really comes alive, but while day-time temperatures can dramatically shoot up, beware sudden, crippling frosts. Also, keep seedlings ticking over on windowsills or in greenhouses, shading them on days when the sun is too fierce.

dahlias

Last year's dahlia tubers should now be sprouting new shoots. As they grow, make sure that they receive sufficient water and light. If it is too dark, the shoots will be weak and spindly. While dahlias are chiefly grown for their autumn colour, the established plants brought on early will add terrific colours from midsummer. New cuttings flower later.

weeding

One of the best reasons for doing the weeding yourself, and not hiring someone else, is that you will quickly start to know the difference between weeds

above Take cuttings from the tips of the stems and put them in a plastic bag. This keeps them safe and moist before planting.

the flower garden

- Plant container-grown shrubs
- Plant herbaceous plants
- Stake herbaceous and border plants
- Feed beds and borders
- Plant hedges
- Plant gladioli and other summer bulbs
- Plant ranunculus tubers
- Mow the lawn regularly from now on
- Make a new lawn from seed or turf
- Buy seeds and bulbs if not already done so
- Plant out sweet peas raised in pots
- Sow sweet peas where they are to flower
- Sow hardy annuals
- Take softwood cuttings
- Plant hanging baskets
- Water newly planted shrubs and trees in dry spells
- Start weeding in earnest
- Divide perennials

above When planting up a hanging basket, standing it on a pot or bucket helps to keep it stable.

and seedlings of plants that you want to keep. If the latter are growing in the wrong place, pot them up and grow them on for planting in the border later.

lawn care

This is a good time of year to level out any hollows in the lawn. The simplest way to tackle any small dips where people might trip over, is by half-filling the hollow with a good loam-based compost (soil mix). The grass will gradually grow up through it, and in from the side. Next month, fill the hollow to the top, and by midsummer the lawn should be firm and flat.

deadheading daffodils

The best way to guarantee a good show of daffodils for next year is to deadhead them, once they have finished flowering. Do not remove the foliage (that continues helping store energy) until nearly dead.

above right Remove the flowerheads of daffodils before the seed has time to develop.

above When replanting divided perennials, dig the soil over first, removing any weeds, and add some well-rotted organic manure.

above Work out where you want your shrubs before planting them, allowing room for them to fill out.

the greenhouse and conservatory

❖ If the greenhouse was not given a thorough spring-clean last month, now is your last chance
❖ Last year's dahlia tubers that are not putting out new shoots, need 18°C (65°F) and gentle watering
❖ Pot up or pot on into larger pots chrysanthemums rooted earlier
❖ Take leaf cuttings of saintpaulias and streptocarpus
❖ Reduce watering for winter-flowering cyclamen
❖ Pot up tomato seedlings into larger pots if necessary, or sow seed of greenhouse crops now
❖ Buy packets of plant labels
❖ Check new growth on pot plants for aphids
❖ Ventilate on warm days, but close shutters in the evening in case of night-time frosts
❖ Provide greenhouse shading to protect plants from high temperatures

above If you do not have a propagator, enclose cuttings in a plastic bag secured with a twist-tie.

late spring

Even late spring can be deceptive. It often seems as though summer has arrived, yet in cold areas there can still be severe late frosts. Take local climate into account before planting any frost-tender plants outdoors. Even with experience it can be a gamble as an untypical season might produce surprises. Judging when frosts are no longer likely is mainly a matter of assessing risk.

It is a good idea to watch when summer bedding is put out in the local parks. These gardeners will have amassed generations of local knowledge of your area, which is by far the best guide.

lemon trees

When buying potted lemon trees (actually shrubs, pruned to whatever size you want, unless you have the space to let them take off), keep them under glass for a while. They dislike a sudden change of temperature. Spray them regularly to provide

above Plant up a herb pot for the summer. Unless the pot is very large, don't try to pack too many herbs into the top. It is better not to plant shrubby plants at the top.

above Half baskets are planted to look good from the front only and do not need to be turned as normal baskets.

above Many plants will grow as a single stem, making spindly growth. If the tip is cut or pinched out, side shoots will develop and the plants will become more bushy.

the flower garden

❖ Plan visits to public gardens and flower shows
❖ Give formal hedges a light trim for shape and to encourage bushiness
❖ Edge flower beds regularly to give a clean shape
❖ Give spring-flowering shrubs a light pruning
❖ Start standing houseplants outdoors when the weather is warm enough
❖ Remove the spring bedding and replace with a lively summer display
❖ Weed regularly in the vegetable garden
❖ Finish practical projects like new ponds
❖ Check that the new growth on climbers is tied in
❖ Seedlings of hardy annuals need thinning out
❖ Save reserve plants of courgettes (zucchini), etc., in case those planted out unexpectedly fail
❖ Check that there are no holes in the bird netting in the kitchen garden
❖ Cordon tomatoes need their side-shoots removing (this does not apply to outdoor bush tomatoes)
❖ Feed lawns and continue to mow regularly

above Marginal aquatics should have a lining around the container so that the soil does not fall through the sides.

humidity, and stand them out in a warm sheltered position next month. Removing the flower buds on young plants diverts the plant's energy into stem growth and leaves. After a couple of years, start to let it fruit.

ponds

As the water warms up, algae will proliferate. Selectively weed it out, leaving some for the tadpoles to hide and feed in. Meanwhile, introduce new plants into the pond, and provide larger containers for established plants where necessary.

border plants

To get new border plants off to a good start, dig a large planting hole and remove any weeds. Most plants also benefit from some well-rotted compost amongst their roots. By the time the whole garden has been planted out, all the beds should have been considerably enriched.

above Use a cloche when hardening off plants raised indoors or in a greenhouse.

above When planting a new shrub, check that the hole is deep enough by placing a stick or cane across it.

the greenhouse and conservatory

* Check that shading is in place
* Damp down greenhouses in hot spells by hosing the floor to add humidity
* Add adjoining water butts for a ready supply of rainwater
* Start creating special pot plant displays
* The early spring-sown bedding plants can be moved to a cold frame for hardening off
* Regularly clean out the greenhouse to prevent the build-up of pests
* Water well any plants grown in greenhouse beds
* Pot up plants, if roots protrude out of existing containers, to the next size pot
* Check that cordon tomatoes have a sturdy support (a cane or secured rope) to climb up

the summer garden

CREATING A SUMMER GARDEN

The summer garden is usually the busiest and most radiant of the gardening year. Colours range from soft pale pastels to bright, flashy "hothouse" colours in many wonderful shades. If you have the right choice of first-rate plants you can keep your floral displays going right to the end of the season. Use big bold groups of your favourite flowers, make sure that you have plenty of scent, highlight contrasts between quiet, flowing shapes and more dramatic, spiky ones, and you will create stunning effects that can last all summer.

left *Crocosmia* 'Lucifer' produces tall, elegant sprays of rich red flowers, which last for several weeks. They stand out well, making a dramatic contrast against the leaves of the flamboyant cannas.

above A subtle, low-key summer planting with a beautiful rhythm of colours and shapes.

EVERYONE CAN CREATE A SUMMER GARDEN with plenty of character and style. With the vast range of plants now available, there are enough bulbs, annuals and perennials to stock even the biggest beds with bright colours and heady fragrances. Mixing these with carefully chosen shrubs, climbers and garden accessories will allow you to experiment with structure, colour and texture and produce superb visual effects.

the right plant in the right place

If you have an empty bed or border, plan your design by deciding upon the overall effect you want to achieve. Do you want an area that is spare, shapely and contemporary, or packed with flowing colour as in a cottage garden?

Choose the style, and then list the best plants that will highlight and dramatize it. If you want a colourful summer display, try a traditional, beautifully free-flowing blend of three or four colours. If your bed or border is circular, place eye-catchingly tall and dramatic plants off-centre towards the middle and then work out to the edge, planting right around it.

If your favoured plant is small, place it near the edge or front of the area. Give each plant space to grow and fill out, even if that means leaving wide, irregular gaps between them in the first few years. The spaces can easily be filled with annuals, sown in the spring, and discarded in the autumn.

Make sure that your preferred colours stand out by placing them next to colours that do not compete. For example, a beautiful, soft gentle lilac will immediately be upstaged if it is placed next to a lipstick red. It is better to use other quiet pastels or greens, making an unobtrusive background. And with a plant that shoots up tall stems or sprays, such as the grass *Stipa gigantea*, which hits 2.5m (8ft) high, place it where it can be lit by the sun or stand out against a dark background.

bedding schemes

Any scheme is a success if it makes you happy. Rules help (for example, stand taller plants towards the back, smaller ones to the front), but they do not have to be adhered to rigidly. Experiment with bright-coloured annuals, for example, you could design a flowerbed with small plants to make a patchwork-quilt effect.

Within flowerbeds you can combine a wide range of colours and textures. Subtle one-colour schemes can be charming. Try combining leaves that are matt and shiny green, olive green and pale green, to form a beautiful mix of tones, and leaves that are feathery, stumpy and round.

You can inject variety and surprise into almost any garden. Place a low-growing bed near a fun, helter-skelter bed, and include plants such as a 2m (6½ft) high *Foeniculum vulgare* 'Purpureum' (bronze fennel) and 2.5m (8ft) high *Helianthus annuus* (sunflowers), with red and yellow *Tropaeolum tuberosum* 'Ken Aslet' climbing up them. Plant yellow-stemmed bamboos with green stripes, such as *Phyllostachys vivax aureocaulis*, to make a startling contrast against dark flowers. Add flashes of colour to any scheme by introducing hanging baskets and containers that give vitality and energy to the summer garden.

above Lilies look especially pleasing among herbaceous plants, which help to hide their stems. They pack plenty of impact into a small space.

left Roses scrambling over an archway are a quintessential ingredient of a summer country garden. As well as adding a delightful froth of blooms, prominently displayed against the sky, the screening effect of the archway gives an air of mystery to the garden.

SUMMER PLANTS

Here is a gallery of the finest summer plants, with everything from the prettiest bulbs and annuals to sensational perennials, shrubs, roses and climbers. The following pages give all the key facts, including how high the plants grow, when they flower, their hardiness rating and, best of all, why you should grow them. With this knowledge, you should be able to select a variety of plants to design a beautiful and visually exciting summer garden.

left The strappy leaves of agapanthus look good with tall grasses. Blue *Agapanthus* 'Ben Hope' forms a wonderful large grouping in front of the masses of *Chionochloa conspicua*.

bulbs

There are some splendid bulbs, corms and tubers for the summer garden. Most are well known, with some surprise inclusions that botanically belong in this section. The stars include richly scented, beautifully coloured lilies and gladioli. Alliums are incredibly popular, especially those called 'drumsticks', which have vertical stems and a ball of colour on top consisting of hundreds of tiny flowers. Dahlias are essential and provide magnificent flashes of colour through the second half of summer, sometimes until the end of autumn.

Summer bulbs are seldom used in large drifts, or with other bedding plants, as are spring bulbs. The majority of them are best treated like ordinary plants in herbaceous or mixed borders, or perhaps used to add foreground interest and colour in a shrub border.

Agapanthus

Commonly known as the lily of the Nile or African blue lily, this genus contains about 10 species of eye-catching clump-forming plants with fleshy roots, and originates from southern Africa. The plants produce strap-shaped, arching leaves and rounded umbels of blue or white flowers, followed by wonderfully decorative seedheads.

below left to right
Agapanthus 'Ben Hope', *A. praecox* subsp. *maximus* 'Albus' and *Allium caeruleum.*

A. 'Ben Hope'

The bell-shaped, rich blue agapanthus flowers make a magnificent display in any colour scheme. The plants flower best when they are overcrowded.
Flowering height 1.2m (4ft)
Flowering time Mid- to late summer
Hardiness Fully hardy

A. praecox subsp. maximus 'Albus'

This forms bold clumps which bear large, white, trumpet-shaped flowers. It is best to grow agapanthus in a sunny border beneath a sunny wall or in pots in a soil-based compost (potting mix), and bring into a dry, frost-free shed in winter.
Flowering height 60–90cm (2–3ft)
Flowering time Mid- to late summer
Hardiness Fully hardy

Allium

This is a large genus of about 700 species of perennial spring-, summer- and autumn-flowering bulbs and rhizomes, from dry and mountainous areas of the northern hemisphere. The genus includes onions, garlic and chives, and the decorative varieties are often known as ornamental onions. They produce short to tall umbels of mauve, pink, blue, white or yellow flowers, usually followed by attractive seedheads.

A. caeruleum

The attractive umbels, composed of 30 to 50 bright blue, star-shaped flowers, sway on slender stems.
Flowering height 20–80cm (8–32in)
Flowering time Early summer
Hardiness Frost hardy, so provide a mulch in winter

A. cristophii

One of the best alliums, with lilac-purple flowers, which have a rich, metallic sheen in sunlight. It is perfect for planting beneath a laburnum arch.
Flowering height 60cm (2ft)
Flowering time Early summer
Hardiness Frost hardy, so provide a mulch in winter

A. hollandicum 'Purple Sensation'

A beautiful allium with umbels consisting of about 50 star-shaped, rich purple flowers. It is perfect for planting beneath a wisteria arch with tall Dutch irises.
Flowering height 90cm (3ft)
Flowering time Early summer
Hardiness Fully hardy

A. karataviense

This allium originates in Central Asia. The rounded umbels consist of 50 or more small, star-shaped, pale pink flowers with purple midribs, borne on stiff stems.

The broad, grey, elliptical, almost horizontal leaves are a special feature of the cultivar.
Flowering height 20cm (8in)
Flowering time Late spring to early summer
Hardiness Fully hardy

A. schubertii

The rounded umbels, which are borne on stiff stems, have inner and outer zones of small, star-shaped, mauve-blue flowers.
Flowering height 40cm (16in)
Flowering time Early summer
Hardiness Fully hardy

above left to right *Allium cristophii, A. karataviense* and *A. schubertii.*

below *Allium hollandicum* 'Purple Sensation' with *Lavandula stoechas.*

Begonia

The genus was named in honour of Michel Bégon
(1638–1710), a French botanist and Governor of
French Canada. It contains about 900 species, some
of which are tuberous-rooted. The tuberous begonias,
whose tubers are dormant in winter, include the
Tuberhybrida, Multiflora and Pendula types, which
derive from species growing in the Andes.

B. 'Double Orange'

This upright begonia has double orange flowers
which are up to 10cm (4in) across, and look
wonderful in mixed summer bedding schemes.
There are also double yellow, pink, red and white
begonias in varying shades.
Flowering height 20cm (8in)
Flowering time Summer
Hardiness Frost tender

B. 'Giant Flowered Pendula Yellow'

The large double and single yellow flowers are 5cm
(2in) across. This pendulous begonia is ideal for
hanging baskets. There is also an attractive 'Giant
Flowered Pendula Orange' as well as pink, white
and red varieties.
Flowering height Trails to 20cm (8in)
Flowering time Summer
Hardiness Frost tender

Canna 'Roi Humbert'

Commonly known as the Indian shot plant, the genus
has 50 species of rhizomatous herbaceous perennials
from moist open areas of forest in Asia and the
tropical parts of North and South America. The
genus name comes from the Greek *kanna*, "reed".
Formerly known as *C.* 'King Humbert', this canna
bears large racemes, 20–30cm (8–12in) long, of
orange-scarlet flowers. They show up well against
the striking reddish bronze, paddle-shaped leaves.
The colour associates well with other bronze
foliage plants such as grasses or *Foeniculum
vulgare* 'Purpureum' (bronze fennel).
Flowering height 2.1m (7ft)
Flowering time Mid- to late summer
Hardiness Half-hardy

Cardiocrinum giganteum

The racemes bear up to 20 fragrant, trumpet-shaped,
cream flowers, streaked with purplish red inside,
which grow up to 15cm (6in) long, followed by
decorative seedheads. A superb plant, it needs plenty
of deep, rich soil where it will not dry out in summer.
It dies after flowering, but new young bulblets will
mature after about four years.
Flowering height 2m (6½ft)
Flowering time Mid- to late summer
Hardiness Fully hardy

Crocosmia 'Lucifer'

The upward-facing, bright red flowers, 5cm (2in) long,
are borne on tall, strong, slightly arching stems. This is
an essential plant in any garden, and it is best grown in
big, bold groups for maximum effect.
Flowering height 90cm (3ft)
Flowering time Late summer
Hardiness Frost hardy, so provide a mulch in winter

Dahlia

The dahlia is one of the showiest flowers in the summer border. It includes about 30 species and some 2,000 cultivars of bushy, tuberous-rooted perennials from mountainous areas of Mexico and Central America. Dahlias are available in many colours, including both strident and pastel shades of yellow, orange, red, deep purple and pink as well as white. They vary in flower size from about 5cm (2in) across, as with the Pompon dahlias, to enormous flowers, almost 30cm (12in) across. They are also available as dwarf patio cultivars and large exhibition dahlias. Nearly all the medium to tall plants will need staking. Dahlia corms are planted out in early summer, dug up, and then kept dryish over winter in a frost-free place.

D. 'Bishop of Llandaff'

A superb dahlia with bright red flowers and contrasting dark foliage.
Flowering height 90cm (3ft)
Flowering time Summer to autumn
Hardiness Half-hardy

D. 'Brilliant Eye'

This is a Pompon flowerhead type. The bright red, rolled petals make neat flowers, which are only 5cm (2in) in diameter. It looks lovely with blue caryopteris.
Flowering height 90cm (3ft)
Flowering time Summer to autumn
Hardiness Fully hardy

D. 'Purple Gem'

A Cactus flowerhead type with long, narrow, pointed, recurved petals that are rich purple. It is good in borders and ideal for cutting.
Flowering height 90cm (3ft)
Flowering time Summer to autumn
Hardiness Half-hardy

left top to bottom *Dahlia* 'Purple Gem', *D.* 'Brilliant Eye' and *D.* 'Bishop of Llandaff'.

Eucomis autumnalis 'White Dwarf'
The small, pale green or white flowers are star-shaped and carried on a dense spike. The flower spike is topped with the familiar crown of bracts.
Flowering height 20–30cm (8–12in)
Flowering time Late summer to autumn
Hardiness Fully hardy

Freesia 'Wintergold'
The fragrant, funnel-shaped flowers are yellow. Use outdoors as a summer bedding plant.
Flowering height 25cm (10in)
Flowering time Corms planted in pots in early spring will flower in midsummer. Those planted out in borders from mid- to late spring will flower in late summer.
Hardiness Half-hardy

Gladiolus
The genus name is derived from the Latin word gladius, "sword", a reference to the shape of the leaves. This is a genus of about 180 species of corms with more than 10,000 hybrids and cultivars. The species are found principally in South Africa, but they also occur in Mediterranean countries, north-western and eastern Africa, Madagascar and western Asia. Apply tomato feed over the summer.

G. 'Charming Beauty'
This hybrid has rose-coloured, funnel-shaped flowers, up to 5cm (2in) across, which are blotched with creamy white. They are borne in succession on slender flower spikes, starting at the bottom. It can survive relatively mild winters in a border, if well mulched to protect the roots from the cold.
Flowering height 60cm (2ft)
Flowering time Summer
Hardiness Half-hardy

G. 'Seraphin'
The pretty, pink, ruffled flowers, up to 5cm (2in) across, each have a white throat and are borne in succession on tall flower spikes. It should be grown in a border and looks lovely near lime-green foliage.
Flowering height 70cm (28in)
Flowering time Summer
Hardiness Half-hardy

above left to right
Gladiolus 'Charming Beauty', *Freesia* 'Wintergold' and *Gladiolus* 'Seraphin'.

below *Eucomis autumnalis* 'White Dwarf'.

above *Lilium lancifolium* 'Tiger Lily'.

below left to right *Lilium candidum, L. 'Enchantment', L. regale* and *L. martagon.*

Lilium

The genus name Lilium is an old Latin name, akin to leirion, which was used by Theophrastus to refer to *Lilium candidum* (Madonna lily), one of the oldest established plants in gardens. There are more than 100 species of bulbs in the genus, which come mainly from scrub and wooded areas of Europe, Asia and North America. They have given rise to scores of excellent hybrids, many with wonderful scents, and there are lilies for sun, shade, acid or alkaline soils.

L. candidum

The Madonna lily has 5 or more white, faintly scented, trumpet-shaped flowers, 5–7.5cm (2–3in) long, with bright yellow anthers. They have a sweet scent and are the only lilies to produce over-wintering basal leaves. They require neutral to alkaline soil.

Flowering height 90cm (3ft)
Flowering time Summer
Hardiness Fully hardy

L. 'Enchantment'

The showy, vivid orange, cup-shaped, unscented flowers, which are marked with dark purple spots, are 12cm (4¾in) across. It is excellent for the border or deep containers, where it can stay for two or three years.

Flowering height 60–90cm (2–3ft)
Flowering time Summer
Hardiness Fully hardy

L. lancifolium

The confident appearance of the tiger lily is a true reflection of its fiery common name, having up to 40, but more usually 5 to 10, pinkish- or reddish-orange, purple-speckled flowers.

Flowering height 60–150cm (2–5ft)
Flowering time Late summer to early autumn
Hardiness Fully hardy

L. martagon

The turkscap lily should be grown in sun or partial shade. It has glossy, nodding, unscented, pink to purplish red flowers with dark purple or maroon spots, which hang from the stems in early to midsummer. The flowers, which are 5cm (2in) across, with sharply recurring petals, were thought to resemble a Turk's cap. It is ideal growing among early summer-flowering shrubs. The naturally occurring *L. martagon* var. *album* is a desirable white form.

Flowering height 90–180cm (3–6ft)
Flowering time Early to midsummer
Hardiness Fully hardy

L. regale

The regal lily, which enjoys full sun, bears large, trumpet-shaped, scented, white flowers. It can be grown in the border, although it needs support. It is excellent growing among deep red or white, late-flowering, old-fashioned roses and is suitable for large, deep pots.

Flowering height 60–180cm (2–6ft)
Flowering time Summer
Hardiness Fully hardy

Sinningia

This genus embraces about 40 species of tuberous perennials and low-growing shrubs from Central and South America. The best-known is the florist's gloxinia. Position them in light or partial shade indoors.

S. 'Etoile de Feu'

Often referred to as *Gloxinia* 'Etoile de Feu', this sinningia produces wide, trumpet-shaped, carmine-pink flowers with wavy paler margins, all summer long.

Flowering height 25cm (10in)
Flowering time Summer indoors
Hardiness Frost tender

S. 'Hollywood'

Often referred to as *Gloxinia* 'Hollywood', this sinningia produces sumptuous, violet, trumpet-shaped flowers. Stand outside in a pot over summer.

Flowering height 25cm (10in)
Flowering time Summer indoors
Hardiness Frost tender

Zantedeschia aethiopica 'Crowborough'

This is commonly called arum lily or calla lily and has large, white, funnel-shaped spathes, which are carried above the glossy leaves. It is found on moist soil around lakes or swamps in southern and eastern Africa.

Flowering height 90cm (3ft)
Flowering time Early to midsummer
Hardiness Frost hardy, so provide a mulch in winter

above left to right
Sinningia 'Etoile de Feu', *Zantedeschia aethiopica* 'Crowborough' and *Sinningia* 'Hollywood'.

above *Alcea rosea.*

below left to right
Ageratum houstonianum
'Blue Danube', *Calendula officinalis* 'Fiesta Gitana' and
Digitalis purpurea f. *albiflora.*

annuals

Every garden needs a lively group of annuals. They provide instant flashes of colour, are ideal for filling gaps between young plants before they flesh out, for replacing spring bedding, and for adding wherever a sudden injection of colour is needed. *Helianthus annuus* (sunflowers), from the dwarf knee-high kind to the magnificent, fast-growing giants, are one of the best when bursting out of a group of bright red perennials, for example. In the spring sow seeds in pots because out in the garden the pigeons demolish the seedlings in seconds.

Ageratum houstonianum

Floss flowers are fluffy half-hardy annuals, mostly in shades of blue. They are ideal for edging a border and are excellent in window boxes. 'Blue Danube' forms compact hummocks of rich lavender-blue flowers, 'Blue Mink' has powder-blue flowers, 'North Star' has warm purplish-blue flowers, 'Pinky Improved' is an unusual dusky pink variety and 'Summer Snow' is a good white form.
Flowering height 15cm (6in)
Flowering time Summer
Hardiness Half-hardy

Alcea

Hollyhocks are such quintessential cottage-garden plants that most gardeners are prepared to put up with their tendency to develop rust for the sake of their spires of mallow-like flowers. Plant them towards the back or middle of a border. The flowers attract plenty of butterflies. Although hollyhocks are included here with annuals, they are in fact biennials, which means that they are sown in one year to flower the next. *A. rosea* has papery-textured flowers, carried the length of tall, felted stems. Named forms include plants in Chater's Double Group, which have peony-like, double flowers in a range of colours, and the impressive 'Nigra', which has rich chocolate-maroon flowers.
Flowering height 2m (6½ ft)
Flowering time Summer
Hardiness Fully hardy

Calendula officinalis

The common name, pot marigold, refers to the culinary use of this hardy annual. The species has cheery, single orange flowers and aromatic, light green leaves. 'Fiesta Gitana' is a compact form, which has orange or yellow (sometimes bicoloured) flowers.
Flowering height 30–60cm (1–2ft)
Flowering time Summer
Hardiness Fully hardy

Cosmos bipinnatus

With one of the longest flowering seasons of any annual, these half-hardies are of unquestioned value, quite apart from the distinction of the glistening flowers and feathery foliage. The compact plants in the Sonata Series produce carmine, pink or white, bowl-shaped flowers. 'Sonata Pink' has soft pink flowers.

Flowering height 90cm (3ft)
Flowering time Summer
Hardiness Half-hardy

Dianthus barbatus

Most dianthus, commonly known as pinks, are perennials or rock garden plants, but there are also a few annuals and the appealing biennial, *D. barbatus* or sweet William, is essential in cottage gardens. Uniquely in the genus, sweet William produces flowers in dense rounded heads. The deliciously-scented flowers can be red, pink or white; some are bicoloured.

Flowering height 60cm (2ft)
Flowering time Early summer
Hardiness Fully hardy

Digitalis

Foxgloves suit any cottage garden-style planting. All have spikes of characteristic, thimble-like flowers in early summer and occasionally produce lesser spikes later on. *D. purpurea* makes a good garden plant, with mounds of soft, grey-green leaves, flushed purple towards the base. It comes in shades of pink, red and purple. The pretty white form is *D. purpurea* f. *albiflora*.

Flowering height 1.5m (5ft)
Flowering time Summer
Hardiness Fully hardy

Gazania

Also known as treasure flowers, most of the garden varieties are tender perennials, grown as annuals in temperate climates. They are ideal for growing along the foot of a wall. 'Daybreak Orange' has orange flowers, which stay open longer than other varieties.

Flowering height 20cm (8in)
Flowering time Summer
Hardiness Half-hardy

Helianthus annuus

Sunflowers are coarse plants, but they can be splendid in isolation. 'Moonwalker' has lemon-yellow petals surrounding chocolate-brown centres. 'Music Box', a good dwarf, has a mixture of cream, yellow to dark red flowers. 'Velvet Queen' has golden-brown leaves.

Flowering height Up to 2.5m (8ft)
Flowering time Summer
Hardiness Fully hardy

above *Cosmos bipinnatus* 'Sonata Pink'.

below left to right
Helianthus annuus 'Velvet Queen', *Dianthus barbatus* and *Gazania* 'Daybreak Orange'.

above left to right *Lobelia erinus* 'Cambridge Blue', *Nemophila menziesii* and *Nigella damascena*.

below *Impatiens walleriana* 'Victoria Rose'.

Impatiens walleriana

Busy Lizzies are invaluable for providing colour in shady spots. Use them at the front of borders, in containers, window boxes, and especially in hanging baskets for a long period of interest. Packed tightly, they will produce a ball of flowers. Double Carousel Mixed produces well-branched plants with double, rose-like flowers in orange, pink, red and white.

Flowering height 23–30cm (9–12in)
Flowering time Summer
Hardiness Frost tender

Lobelia erinus

These perennial compact forms (grown as annuals) are the mainstay of park bedding schemes, while a hanging basket would be virtually unthinkable without the trailing kinds. Lobelias are among the few shade-tolerant annuals. Most are blue, although there are also selections in other colours. The compact 'Cambridge Blue', which is suitable for bedding, has mauve-blue flowers. Trailing varieties suitable for hanging baskets include those in the Cascade Series. 'Sapphire' has rich blue flowers with white eyes.

Flowering height 10–15cm (4–6in)
Flowering time Summer to autumn
Hardiness Fully hardy

Nemophila menziesii

These hardy annuals are commonly known as baby blue-eyes, because of their delightful, sky-blue, cup-shaped flowers with white centres. They should be planted near the edge of a border or in a container or window box where the flowers can be fully appreciated. In summer this carpeting species can be completely smothered in blooms.

Flowering height 15cm (6in)
Flowering time Summer
Hardiness Fully hardy

Nigella damascena

Love-in-a-mist is a charming, elegant annual, and is a dainty cottage-garden stalwart, almost as attractive when the seedheads develop as when it is in flower; the feathery foliage is a definite bonus. They are very easy to grow. The species is the parent of the garden strains. 'Dwarf Moody Blue' is a compact form, which can be used to make a temporary low "hedge" at the margin of a border. The flowers are sky-blue. The popular 'Miss Jekyll' has bright blue, semi-double flowers. The rarer, desirable 'Miss Jekyll Alba' is white.

Flowering height 20cm (8in) to 45cm (18in)
Flowering time Summer
Hardiness Fully hardy

Oenothera biennis

Evening primrose is a stately annual or biennial, and produces a succession of flowers over the summer months that are valuable for attracting butterflies and other beneficial insects into the garden.

Flowering height 90cm (3ft)
Flowering time Summer
Hardiness Fully hardy

Papaver somniferum

The opium poppy has blue-green leaves, and produces pink, purplish, red or white flowers, followed by striking seedheads. Double forms have distinctive ruffled petals. 'Hen and Chickens' has pink flowers, but is really grown for its larger than average seedheads which can be dried for winter decoration.

Flowering height 90cm (3ft)
Flowering time Summer
Hardiness Fully hardy

Tagetes

Commonly known as marigolds, they are among the easiest of half-hardy annuals to grow, and provide a long-lasting display. There are two large groups, African marigolds and French marigolds. African marigolds tend to be taller and less spreading than the French.

Flowering height 20–45cm (8–18in)
Flowering time Summer
Hardiness Half-hardy

T. tenuifolia

These half-hardy marigolds are bushy and produce domes of flowers. Plants of the Gem Series have single flowers in shades of yellow or orange, marked with darker colours. 'Golden Gem' is a selection with golden-yellow flowers.

Flowering height 15–23cm (6–9in)
Flowering time Late spring to early summer
Hardiness Half-hardy

Tropaeolum

Nasturtiums are easy-to-grow, half-hardy annuals, with orange, yellow or red flowers. Some strains make large plants with trailing stems, which are useful for providing quick cover, although the large leaves tend to mask the flowers. The more compact forms are good for bedding. The young leaves and the flowers are edible. *T. majus* is a quick-growing climber which can spread to 2.5m (8ft).

Flowering height Up to 2.5m (8ft)
Flowering time Summer
Hardiness Half-hardy

above *Tropaeolum majus.*

below left to right
Oenothera biennis, Papaver somniferum and *Tagetes tenuifolia* 'Golden Gem' in the Jubilee Series.

perennials

Choose plenty of perennials because they will never let you down. They keep coming up, year after year, need minimal maintenance, and can be used to create all kinds of mood, whether you want a soft, romantic garden or one that is flamboyantly smart and vibrant. They provide a fantastic range of colours, shapes and sizes, and include plenty of plants on most people's 'Top 10 Beauties'. The hardy geraniums, irises, euphorbias, lupins and poppies all bring the garden alive. They smother summer weeds, and can easily be divided in the spring if you need extra plants to give a display even more impact.

above *Campanula latiloba* 'Percy Piper'.

below left to right
Campanula lactiflora,
Alstroemeria 'Morning Star'
and *Alchemilla mollis.*

Alchemilla mollis

Lady's mantle is an essential garden plant. It is an excellent filler for gaps in borders and the frothy, lime-green, scented flowers, also good for cutting, blend with almost everything else. It makes good ground cover but can self-seed invasively. To prevent this from happening, cut off the flowers as they fade (which will also encourage further flowers).
Flowering height 50cm (20in)
Flowering time Summer
Hardiness Fully hardy

Alstroemeria

Peruvian lily, or lily of the Incas, is an exquisite plant, long associated with cottage gardens. Excellent in a warm, sunny border, in cold areas they need the shelter of a wall. Leave them undisturbed after planting; they may take some years to establish. *A.* 'Morning Star' is a hybrid with rich purplish-pink flowers fading to yellow and flecked with brown from midsummer to autumn.
Flowering height 45cm (18in)
Flowering time Summer
Hardiness Frost hardy, so provide a mulch in winter

Campanula

Bellflowers are stalwarts of the summer border and combine easily with a huge range of plants, especially roses. Tough and easy to grow, their refreshing blue tones are a valuable addition to almost any scheme. *C. lactiflora* is commonly known as the milky bellflower. There are a number of desirable forms of this Caucasian species, all flowering in summer. The tall, sturdy stems make them excellent for giving height to a border. 'Prichard's Variety' has violet-blue flowers.
Flowering height 1.2m (4ft)
Flowering time Summer
Hardiness Fully hardy

Chrysanthemum

There are scores of showy chrysanthemums for the garden, providing a wide range of marvellous colours. They excel in the second half of summer, and in early autumn. That is when they really give the garden a lift. You can grow chrysanthemums for exhibitions with enormous blooms, but that requires all kinds of specialist techniques. For most gardeners, chrysanthemums are far better out in the garden than on greenhouse benches, where they provide fulsome sprays of mauve, red, white, yellow and orange, in flowers that range from large balls, to open stars like large daisies, to spidery shapes with thin dangly petals. Every garden should have one. Patio gardens, cottage gardens, architectural displays, and even modern gardens with all kinds of geometric shapes benefit from the late-season boost of colour and warmth that chrysanthemums provide.

C. hybrids

The following is just a small selection, and all are hardy unless otherwise stated. 'Bronze Elegance' has light bronze, pompon flowers. 'Curtain Call' has anemone-centred, orange flowers. 'George Griffiths' is an early-flowering half-hardy form, with large, deep red, fully reflexed flowers; it is often grown for exhibition. 'Glamour' has warm, reddish-pink pompon flowers. 'Mei-kyo' is an early-flowering plant with pink pompon flowers. 'Pennine Oriel', an early-flowering plant, has anemone-centred, white flowers. 'Primrose

Allouise' is an early-flowering half-hardy sport of 'White Allouise', with weather-resistant, incurving, soft yellow flowers. 'Southway Swan' has single flowers, with silvery pink petals surrounding yellow-green centres. 'Taffy' has rich bronze-orange flowers.
Flowering height Up to 2m (6½ft)
Flowering time Summer to autumn
Hardiness Mostly fully hardy

Delphinium

These magnificent, stately plants grow in a range of colours that few other perennials can match: primrose-yellow, cream, white, pale and dark blue, mauve, pink and deep purple. A traditional herbaceous border would be unthinkable without them. There are many excellent garden hybrids, but only a few can be described here. Elatum Group plants have almost flat flowers in dense, upright spikes; Belladonna Group plants have branched stems and loose sprays of flowers. 'Blue Nile' (Elatum) is a classic pale blue delphinium. 'Casablanca' (Belladonna), which has pure white flowers with yellow centres, is an excellent choice for a pale planting. 'Clifford Sky' (Elatum) has Wedgwood-blue flowers. 'Finsteraarhorn' (Elatum) has cobalt-blue flowers touched with purple. 'Mighty Atom' (Elatum) has solidly packed spikes of semi-double, lavender-blue flowers with brown eyes.
Flowering height 1.2–1.5m (4–5ft)
Flowering time Summer
Hardiness Mostly fully hardy

above left to right
A double-flowered, reflexed florist's spray chrysanthemum, C. 'Southway Swan' and C. 'Primrose Allouise'.

below *Delphinium* 'Clifford Sky'.

above left to right
Dianthus 'Louise's Choice',
D. 'Mrs Sinkins' and *D.*
'Riccardo'.

below *Dianthus*
'Dawlish Joy'.

Dianthus

Commonly known as carnations or pinks, these bright, highly attractive plants give an exquisite touch, whether they are grown in special containers, for example old kitchen sinks or Victorian chimney pots, or right at the front of a border. The more you deadhead them, removing the faded flowers, the more they keep on flowering. Group together various different colours, and make sure that you grow some of the highly scented kind, for example the old-fashioned white, 'Mrs Sinkins'. All need wall-to-wall sun and free-draining soil. Avoid clay.

All the following are hardy. 'Bovey Belle' has double purple flowers. 'Brympton Red' has fragrant, crimson flowers with darker marbling. The scented flowers of 'Dad's Favourite' are white laced with maroon, with dark centres. 'Dawlish Joy' has variegated pink flowers. 'Doris', a bicolour, has pale pink flowers with maroon centres. 'Excelsior' has large-petalled, pink flowers; the flowers of 'Freckles' are salmon-pink, delicately blotched with red. 'Gran's Favourite' has clove-scented, white flowers laced with maroon. 'Joy' has salmon-pink flowers. 'Louise's Choice' has crimson-laced pink flowers. The miniature 'Mendlesham Maid' has white flowers with frilly petal edges. The bicolour 'Monica Wyatt' has phlox-pink flowers with ruby centres; 'Mrs Sinkins' is fragrant, with double, white, fringed flowers; 'Riccardo' is a border carnation with red and white flowers; 'White Ladies' has clove-scented, double, white flowers, purer in colour than 'Mrs Sinkins'.
Flowering height 45cm (18in)
Flowering time Summer
Hardiness Mostly fully hardy

Eryngium

Sea holly is a spiky, stiffly branched, architectural plant, perhaps best given space to make its own statement, ideally in a gravel garden. It will also integrate in mixed borders, providing an excellent contrast to softer plants. Some are biennials. This striking plant has deeply cut, bluish-grey leaves, veined white, and spiky steel-blue cones of flowers.
Flowering height 60cm (2ft), usually
Flowering time Midsummer
Hardiness Fully hardy

Euphorbia myrsinites

This succulent-looking species needs a degree of pampering. Grow in full sun, in a gravel garden with excellent drainage, in full sun or in troughs. The thick, almost triangular leaves are blue-green. The long-lasting, greenish-yellow flowers fade to pink.
Flowering height 15cm (6in)
Flowering time Early summer
Hardiness Fully hardy

Geranium

It would be difficult to overestimate the value of these plants. Easy to grow, spreading rapidly and combining happily with a range of other plants, they are excellent in informal, cottage-garden schemes, associating particularly well with most roses. They make excellent ground cover without being invasive.

G. 'Ann Folkard'

A fine plant, this bears a succession of magenta flowers, with blackish centres and veining, throughout summer. Early in the season the flowers are pleasingly offset by yellowish leaves, but they usually turn green by midsummer.
Flowering height 30cm (12in)
Flowering time Early summer
Hardiness Fully hardy

G. 'Johnson's Blue'

A plant for every garden, this hybrid has clear blue flowers over mounds of copious green leaves.
Flowering height 30cm (12in)
Flowering time Early summer
Hardiness Fully hardy

G. phaeum

The flowers, borne on elegant, wiry stems, are an unusual shade of deep, almost blackish, purple.
Flowering height 60cm (2ft)
Flowering time Early summer
Hardiness Fully hardy

above *Eryngium.*

below left to right
Geranium 'Ann Folkard',
*G. phaeum, Euphorbia
myrsinites* and *Geranium*
'Johnson's Blue'.

Hemerocallis

Daylilies have trumpet-like flowers and are of great value in gardens. They make excellent border plants, rapidly forming large, vigorous clumps. Although the individual flowers last only a day (hence the common name), they are freely produced over a long period, and the grassy foliage is always appealing. Small daylilies are excellent for edging a border; the larger kinds consort happily with hostas and roses of all kinds. The species is tough enough for a wild garden.

H. hybrids

'Jake Russell' has golden-yellow flowers with a velvety sheen in mid- to late summer. The vigorous 'Little Grapette' has deep purple flowers in midsummer. 'Lusty Leland' produces an abundance of scarlet and yellow flowers over a long period in summer. 'Prairie Blue Eyes' is semi-evergreen with lavender-purple flowers in midsummer. 'Scarlet Orbit' has bright red flowers with yellow-green throats in midsummer. 'Stafford', one of the best of its colour range, has rich scarlet flowers with yellow throats in midsummer.
Flowering height 60cm (2ft)
Flowering time Summer
Hardiness Fully hardy

Iris

This large genus also includes bulbs. The plants described here are perennials. I. 'Blue Eyed Brunette' has distinctive rich red-brown flowers with gold beards. I. pallida is an excellent blue for the border. The warm lavender-blue flowers are good for cutting.
Flowering height 90cm (3ft)
Flowering time Early summer
Hardiness Fully hardy

Kniphofia

Some people think of red hot pokers as vulgar, but there is no denying the impact that they can have in a garden with their luminous torch-like flowers. K. 'Alcazar', an archetypal poker, has bright red flowers.

Flowering height Up to 1.5m (5ft)
Flowering time Early, mid- or late summer
Hardiness Mostly fully hardy

Lupinus

With their tall spires of pea flowers in a range of colours (some being bicoloured), lupins are essential for giving height to borders in early to midsummer.
Flowering height 90cm (3ft)
Flowering time Midsummer
Hardiness Fully hardy

Monarda

Bergamot is an excellent border plant that bears showy heads of hooded flowers in a range of clear colours. They are ideal for a mixed or herbaceous border. 'Alba' has white flowers. M. didyma, or sweet bergamot, is often included in herb gardens.
Flowering height 90cm (3ft)
Flowering time Mid- to late summer
Hardiness Fully hardy

Papaver orientale

Most of the perennial poppies grown in gardens are descended from this species. They are usually grouped under P. orientale for practical reasons; they all produce large, bowl-shaped flowers. 'Effendi' has orange-red flowers. 'Khedive' has pale pink flowers.
Flowering height 90cm (3ft)
Flowering time Early summer
Hardiness Fully hardy

Pelargonium

With an endless succession of cheerful flowers, in shades of white, pink and crimson, pelargoniums are the archetypal summer plant. These (usually) evergreen tender perennials can be grown in hanging baskets, containers, window boxes or in summer bedding.
Flowering height Up to 45cm (18in)
Flowering time Summer
Hardiness Frost tender

opposite from top, left to right Hemerocallis 'Jake Russell', H. 'Little Grapette', H. 'Stafford', Iris 'Blue Eyed Brunette', I. pallida, Kniphofia 'Alcazar', Lupins, Papaver orientale 'Khedive' and Monarda didyma.

below Pelargonium 'Irene'.

above left to right
Calluna vulgaris 'Tib', *Cistus* 'Sunset' and *Buddleja alternifolia.*

below *Buddleja davidii* 'Nanho Blue'.

shrubs

A good choice of shrubs will give you a strong garden structure with green leaves all year, plenty of flowers attracting butterflies and bees, and some fantastically strong scents. Most are very easy to look after, only needing trimming and shaping. If you have room, and allow them to grow, many will eventually reach the size of small trees. If you only have room for one, choose a mock orange (*Philadelphus*) for its richly perfumed white flowers.

Buddleja
The heavily scented flowers of these medium-to-large deciduous shrubs are irresistible to butterflies. They are reliable plants for the back of a border.

B. alternifolia
This handsome plant has pendent racemes of deliciously scented mauve flowers in early summer. Pruning easily controls its size. The form 'Argentea' is even more desirable. It has silver-grey leaves and is very effective as a standard and specimen.
Height 4m (13ft)
Flowering time Summer
Hardiness Fully hardy

B. davidii
Commonly called the butterfly bush, this bears long spikes of fragrant, usually mauve flowers. It is essential in a wild or ecological garden because of its attraction for butterflies. There are several selections, all of which can be pruned hard in late winter to early spring, including 'Black Knight', which has deep reddish-purple flowers, 'Nanho Blue' with rich lavender-blue flowers, and 'Peace', which is a reliable white selection.
Height 3m (10ft)
Flowering time Mid- to late summer
Hardiness Fully hardy

Calluna
This genus of heathers consists of a single species, but there are a huge number of cultivars, all evergreen and producing their spikes of bell-shaped flowers between midsummer and late autumn. Some also have coloured foliage, which provides interest over a longer period. Heathers are excellent in containers and rock gardens. *C. vulgaris* 'Tib' is the earliest double cultivar to flower, with racemes of small, double, cyclamen-purple flowers and dark green leaves.
Height Up to 60cm (2ft)
Flowering time Summer to late autumn
Hardiness Fully hardy

Cistus

Often called sun rose or rock rose, in Mediterranean countries these scrubby evergreen shrubs cover large areas of open ground, as heathers do in northern Europe. The flowers, which have a papery texture, like poppies, are short-lived, but follow one another in quick succession at the height of summer. They are perfect in a gravel garden, basking in the reflected heat from the stones, and combine well with shrubby herbs. This is a good compact shrub for a small garden.

Height 90cm (3ft)
Flowering time Early to midsummer
Hardiness Fully hardy

Daboecia

This genus of heathers contains two evergreen species: *D. cantabrica* and *D. x scotica*. They are best grown *en masse* in an open situation or in beds with other heathers or conifers. *D. cantabrica* 'Atropurpurea' has pinkish-purple flowers and bronze-tinted foliage.

Height 40cm (16in)
Flowering time Early summer to mid-autumn
Hardiness Fully hardy

Fuchsia

There are thousands of hybrids of this deservedly popular genus. They flower over a long period. Some have small, dainty flowers but others are more flamboyant. Plant them in beds and borders, as wall shrubs, and in containers and hanging baskets. *F.* 'Caroline' is a half-hardy fuchsia with purplish corollas and creamy pink sepals. It is an upright plant, about 90cm (3ft) high. *F.* 'Gay Parasol' is a tender bedding fuchsia with dark red-purple corollas and sepals that are ivory, about 90cm (3ft) high. *F.* 'Royal Velvet' is a tender bedding fuchsia with large double flowers with luminous deep purple corollas and crimson sepals. It makes an exceptionally good standard and is about 75cm (30in) high.

Hardy hybrids include *F.* 'Army Nurse', with semi-double, blue-violet and deep carmine-red flowers. It makes an excellent standard. *F.* 'Hawkshead' is a popular cultivar, with single, pinkish-white flowers, which are tinged green.

Height Up to 90cm (3ft)
Flowering time Summer
Hardiness Fully hardy to frost tender

above *Daboecia cantabrica* 'Atropurpurea'.

below left to right *Fuchsia* 'Caroline', *F.* 'Royal Velvet' and *F.* 'Gay Parasol'.

Hebe

These are grown for their summer flowers, which are highly attractive to bees, and for their foliage. Compact types are good in containers.

H. 'Blue Clouds'

This excellent hybrid has long spikes of bluish-mauve flowers from early summer until well into autumn.
Height 90cm (3ft)
Flowering time Summer to autumn
Hardiness Fully hardy

H. 'Great Orme'

An elegant hybrid, this has narrow green leaves and spikes of pale pink flowers, ageing to white.
Height 1.5m (5ft)
Flowering time Summer to autumn
Hardiness Frost hardy

Hydrangea

They are among the few deciduous shrubs that thrive in containers. Hydrangea flowerheads take a number of forms: pretty lacecaps have a central mass of tiny fertile flowers surrounded by larger sterile flowers; mopheads (hortensias) have domed heads of sterile flowers only.

H. arborescens

Commonly known as Sevenbark, this is less widely grown than its named selections, the loveliest of which is 'Annabelle', which produces large, cream-coloured flowerheads.
Height 1.5m (5ft)
Flowering time Late summer
Hardiness Fully hardy

H. macrophylla

The stiffly growing shrub 'Altona' has flowers that are cerise-pink on alkaline soils and mid-blue on acid soils.
Height 1–1.5m (3–5ft)
Flowering time Mid- to late summer
Hardiness Fully hardy

Lavandula angustifolia

Old English lavender has grey-green leaves and scented blue-grey flowers. The many selections include 'Hidcote' (syn. *L.* 'Hidcote Blue'), which has deep lavender-blue flowers; 'Munstead' which has soft, lilac-blue flowers; and the strong-growing 'Rosea' has pink flowers. All need full sun and well-drained soil.
Height 60cm (2ft)
Flowering time Early to late summer
Hardiness Fully hardy

Perovskia

Russian sage produces a sheaf of whitened stems with small, mauve-blue flowers. It is excellent in a gravel or Mediterranean garden. *P.* 'Blue Spire' has silver-blue, deeply cut leaves and spires of rich blue flowers.

Height 90cm (3ft)
Flowering time Late summer
Hardiness Fully hardy

Philadelphus 'Belle Etoile'

The scent of the mock orange is unmistakable and almost cloyingly sweet when it hangs in the air in early summer. Most of the plants in cultivation are hybrids of garden origin. Grow them as a fragrant backdrop to a mixed border.

Height 1.5m (5ft)
Flowering time Midsummer
Hardiness Fully hardy

Potentilla

These neat, hardy, deciduous shrubs bear masses of flat, open flowers throughout the summer, in shades of red, orange, yellow, pink and white. They need sun and do well in rock gardens or at the front of borders. *P. fruticosa* is the best-known species; its many cultivars include 'Medicine Wheel Mountain', which has yellow flowers.

Height 90cm (3ft)
Flowering time Summer
Hardiness Fully hardy

Rosmarinus officinalis

This aromatic shrub has dark green, narrow leaves and mauve-blue flowers in summer. 'Lady in White' has white flowers. 'Miss Jessop's Upright' (syn. 'Fastigiatus') is an upright form with light purplish-blue flowers.

Height 1.5m (5ft)
Flowering time Summer
Hardiness Borderline hardy

Santolina chamaecyparis

Cotton lavender is a mound-forming shrub with finely dissected silvery leaves. It has lemon-yellow flowers in midsummer, but is principally valued as a foliage plant.

Height 60cm (2ft)
Flowering time Summer
Hardiness Fully hardy

above *Santolina chamaecyparis.*

below left to right *Potentilla fruticosa* 'Medicine Wheel Mountain', *Perovskia* 'Blue Spire', *Rosmarinus officinalis* and *Philadelphus* 'Belle Etoile'.

above *Rosa* 'Albertine'.

below left to right
Rosa 'Fragrant Cloud',
R. 'Elizabeth Harkness'
and *R.* 'Sexy Rexy'.

roses

The rose is the quintessential summer flower. Many modern varieties combine a cast-iron constitution with an unrivalled length of flowering. Some are dainty and elegant, others richly coloured show-stoppers, and many are deliciously fragrant. Besides their value as climbers and ramblers, and in beds and borders, some can be used for ground cover, while those with a neat, compact habit are ideal for growing in containers.

Rosa 'Albertine'

A vigorous rambling rose with fully double, light pink flowers, which appear in a single flush in midsummer, opening from copper-tinted buds. The rich, distinctive scent of this rose has assured its continuing popularity.
Height 5m (16ft)
Flowering time Summer
Hardiness Fully hardy

R. 'Elizabeth Harkness'

This large-flowered rose, of upright habit, was introduced in 1969. It produces shapely, fully double, fragrant, ivory-white flowers that flush pink as they age. The leaves are semi-glossy. 'Elizabeth Harkness' is good in beds and for cut flowers.

Height 75cm (2½ft)
Flowering time Summer
Hardiness Fully hardy

R. 'Escapade'

A cluster-flowered rose, of freely branching habit, introduced in 1967. The semi-double, sweetly scented flowers are of unique colouring: borne in clusters from summer to autumn, they are soft lilac-pink, opening flat to reveal white centres and golden stamens. The leaves are glossy bright green. A disease-resistant rose, 'Escapade' is good for cutting and in mixed plantings.
Height 1.2m (4ft)
Flowering time Summer
Hardiness Fully hardy

R. 'Fragrant Cloud'

A large-flowered rose, of sturdy, branching habit. The fully double, richly scented, bright geranium-red flowers, ageing to purplish-red, are carried from summer to autumn. The leaves are leathery, and dark green. It is an outstanding rose that can be used in bedding and for cut flowers.
Height 75cm (2½ft)
Flowering time Summer
Hardiness Fully hardy

R. 'Golden Showers'

This climbing rose is an enduring favourite of many gardeners. It produces clusters of double, lightly scented, yellow flowers. The flowers lack distinction, having few petals, but the reliability of this rose in a variety of situations has ensured its popularity.

Height 3m (10ft)
Flowering time Summer to autumn
Hardiness Fully hardy

R. 'Ingrid Bergman'

A large-flowered rose, of upright, branching habit. The fully double, only lightly scented flowers are deep red and the leaves are glossy dark green. It is good for cutting, bedding and containers.

Height 75cm (2½ft)
Flowering time Summer to autumn
Hardiness Fully hardy

R. 'Just Joey'

A large-flowered rose, of upright, branching habit. It has elegant, long, shapely buds that open to lightly scented, fully double, coppery orange-pink flowers with slightly ruffled petals. The matt dark green leaves are tinted red on emergence. 'Just Joey' is an outstanding rose, valued for its freedom of flowering, general disease-resistance and versatility in the garden, besides the unusual colour of the blooms.

Height 75cm (2½ft)
Flowering time Summer
Hardiness Fully hardy

R. 'Louise Odier'

A Bourbon rose, introduced in 1851, that is suitable for training as a climber and is best with some support. From midsummer to autumn it produces clusters of cupped, fully double, strongly scented, lilac-tinted, warm pink flowers. The leaves are greyish-green.

Height 2.3m (7½ft)
Flowering time Midsummer to autumn
Hardiness Fully hardy

R. 'Sexy Rexy'

A cluster-flowered rose, of upright habit, that was introduced in 1984. Clusters of shapely, fully double, lightly scented, clear light pink flowers are produced in summer and into autumn. A versatile rose, 'Sexy Rexy' is excellent for garden use, in containers, and as a cut flower.

Height 60cm (2ft)
Flowering time Summer to autumn
Hardiness Fully hardy

top *Rosa* 'Louise Odier'.

above *Rosa* 'Escapade'.

below left to right *Rosa* 'Golden Showers', R. 'Ingrid Bergman' and R. 'Just Joey'.

above *Bougainvillea.*

below left to right
Clematis 'Mrs Cholmondeley',
C. 'Royalty' and *C.* 'Bees'
Jubilee'.

climbers

These versatile plants can be used to romp up trees, cover walls, twist round pillars and poles or cover a trellis to produce stunning masses of colour and scent.

Bougainvillea

These evergreen climbers are grown for the brightly coloured bracts that surround their insignificant flowers. The spiny stems have to be tied to a trellis. In warm climates they are impressive over large pergolas or cascading down banks. Combining them with *Trachelospermum jasminoides* will provide the scent they lack.
Height Up to 12m (40ft)
Flowering time Summer to autumn (bracts)
Hardiness Half-hardy to frost tender

Clematis

There is a superb range of summer-flowering clematis in many shades and colours. Large-flowered hybrids are excellent on walls and fences; others are good for growing through bushes, over buildings and architectural features.

C. 'Bees' Jubilee'

A large-flowered clematis. In spring it produces masses of single, deep mauve-pink flowers, 13cm (5in) across, that lighten with age, each sepal having a darker central bar; the anthers are light brown. A second flush of smaller flowers appears in mid- to late summer.

'Bees' Jubilee', a compact and reliable clematis, is similar to the more commonly grown 'Nelly Moser'.
Height 2.5m (8ft)
Flowering time Summer
Hardiness Fully hardy

C. 'Jackmanii Superba'

A large-flowered clematis that produces an abundance of velvety, rich purple flowers, 15cm (6in) across, with light brown anthers.
Height 3m (10ft)
Flowering time Mid- to late summer
Hardiness Fully hardy

C. 'Mrs Cholmondeley'

It has single, pale lavender-blue flowers, to 13cm (5in) across. 'Mrs Cholmondeley' has one of the longest flowering seasons of all clematis.
Height 3m (10ft)
Flowering time Summer
Hardiness Fully hardy

C. 'Royalty'

In late spring to summer this large-flowered clematis produces an abundance of semi-double, purplish-mauve flowers, 15cm (6in) across, with pale yellow anthers. Later flowers, from midsummer to autumn, are smaller and single. 'Royalty' tolerates any aspect.
Height 1.8m (6ft)
Flowering time From late spring to summer
Hardiness Fully hardy

Jasminum officinale

This is a twining, highly-scented climber with small white flowers. 'Aureum' has leaves splashed with yellow.
Height 5m (16ft)
Flowering time Summer
Hardiness Frost hardy

Lathyrus grandiflorus

This suckering species has glowing pinkish-purple flowers in summer and is good in a wild garden.
Height 2m (6½ft)
Flowering time Summer
Hardiness Frost hardy

Lonicera periclymenum

A common woodlander in Europe, the honeysuckle has scented, creamy-white flowers in summer. There are three excellent forms. 'Belgica' has pink and red flowers, followed by red berries. 'Graham Thomas' bears copper-tinted, creamy flowers. 'Serotina' has purple and red flowers.
Height 3m (10ft)
Flowering time Mid- and late summer
Hardiness Fully hardy

Passiflora caerulea

Passionflowers are highly distinctive climbers, with ten outer petals surrounding a crown of central filaments, inside which are the prominent stamens and styles. The summer flowers are white, with the filaments banded blue, white and purple. The form 'Constance Elliot' has fragrant, creamy white flowers with red stigmas.
Height 6m (20ft)
Flowering time Summer to autumn
Hardiness Borderline hardy

Solanum crispum

These delightful climbers deserve to be better known. They produce an abundance of potato flowers over a long period and are generally easy to grow in well-drained soil in full sun. The best form 'Glasnevin', which can be evergreen, has deep blue flowers, with prominent central yellow 'beaks', which are carried in clusters over many weeks in summer. *Solanum jasminoides* 'Album' has lovely yellow-centred, white flowers.
Height 5m (16ft)
Flowering time Summer
Hardiness Borderline hardy

above left to right
Jasminum officinale 'Aureum', *Solanum crispum* 'Glasnevin' and *Lonicera periclymenum*.

below left to right
Clematis 'Jackmanii Superba', *Lathyrus grandiflorus* and *Passiflora caerulea*.

SUMMER DISPLAYS

A summer garden in full bloom is delightful. Dominant colours come and go with perennial poppies and dahlias flinging out brightly coloured flowers and then fading away. Foxglove spires pop up among shrubs, and hardy geraniums flower in blue, pink, red and white, while old-fashioned roses unleash beautiful displays in midsummer. The key to success is making sure that you have a succession of flowering plants, always providing surprises, from early summer until autumn sets in.

left A lively informal border display, mixing shrubs, perennials and biennials, with lilac-blue perovskia, pink and cream hollyhocks, buddleia and purple verbena.

scented gardens

above left A simple trellis arbour and wooden bench are surrounded by heavily scented plants, including a free-flowing jasmine.

above right A window box planted with nicotiana and heliotrope, here in a sophisticated all-white colour scheme, will bring the sweet scents of the flowers into the home.

right A pretty, fragrant border of *Lilium regale* (regal lily), roses and lavender.

Summer gardens need plenty of scent. Roses are always favourites, but there are many more rich, intriguing scents on offer. With the right choice you can have the fragrance of pineapple (from *Cytisus battandieri*), marzipan (*Heliotropium*), and even chocolate (*Cosmos atrosanguineus*). Mix scented plants with showy but less fragrant flowers such as crocosmia and agapanthus to create pretty displays.

sheltered corners

When growing scented plants, you want the perfume to hang in the air. It is no use growing fragrant honeysuckles, lilies and daphnes in open or windy parts of the garden where the scent will get blown away. You need to grow them in sheltered sites in full sun, where the plants will flower well, and where you can sit and enjoy them to the full. Good sites are under windows – climbers such as roses and jasmine can even reach bedroom windows – and near doors. A must for patios where you sit outside in the evening is night-scented stock (*Matthiola bicornis*), which is easy to grow and at dusk its intoxicating perfume hangs heavy in the air.

One of the best lilies you can grow is *Lilium regale*. Plant it in the autumn, and they will come up every summer bearing large, exciting, white trumpet-shaped flowers with the most amazing scent. They need to grow among other perennials, for example hardy geraniums and penstemons, which can take over once the lilies finish flowering.

Slugs are the main enemy of lilies, biting through their stems. If you cannot eradicate them in your garden grow the lilies in pots, and put horticultural gravel on the soil surface. In flowerbeds, scatter grit around the lilies, and ensure your pond has plenty of hungry frogs, which devour the slugs at night.

extra summer scents

Most of the daphnes flower in the spring, but one that flowers sporadically through the summer is the sweetly-scented *D. tangutica*. Lilacs are big shrubs and trees, and there are some first-rate choices in the

4m (13ft) high range. *Syringa pubescens* subsp. *microphylla* 'Superba' keeps flowering, in bursts, all summer. *S. x josiflexa* 'Bellicent' (pink flowers) is small enough, at 3m (10ft) high, for most gardens, and is heaven in early summer. Other scented shrubs include *Philadelphus* (mock orange), while *Nicotiana sylvestris* (tobacco plant) is a good choice of annual. *Oenothera biennis* is an excellent biennial that self-seeds round the garden. The yellow flowers release their scent in the evening.

highly scented climbers

The top scented summer climbers include roses, honeysuckle and jasmine. One of the best roses is the beautiful bright red 'Crimson Glory, Climbing', which has pointed buds, opening to wide, velvet-like petals with a heavy, rich scent. At 5m (16ft) high, most gardens have room for one. 'Gloire de Dijon' is a buff yellow, and grows equally high, and if you want one of the darkest of the scented climbing roses, 'Guinee' (also 5m) is a striking rich crimson. Put any of these reds near the white jasmine, *Jasminum officinale*, for a marvellous show. The latter needs to twist and twine around a support, such as a drainpipe up the side of the house or an old, stout tree.

above left A mature honeysuckle will perfume an enclosed patio area during early summer evenings.

above right *Gladiolus communis byzantinus* and *Cistus purpureus* make an audacious pink colour combination in the garden. Combine with pink, scented roses to add fragrance to the border.

left The soft pink climbing roses give out a heady summer scent and create an interesting effect against the pastel pink and blue fence.

right In a small garden, make every corner earn its keep. This wooden and brick unit provides seating and can be filled with flowers and herbs.

below Clematis-clad, bamboo trelliswork with symmetrical patterning creates a perfect backdrop to a border.

garden ornament

The best summer gardens are kept lively and interesting not just by the choice of plants, but by using a wide range of creative ornaments. These can be expensive and elaborate, low-key and rustic – whatever will best highlight the style of the garden and emphasize its personality. If you choose attractively shaped items, they will look good when they are offset with summer flowers, and really stand out during winter when most plants are taking a rest.

The range of objects can include everything from beautiful circular tables made of wood or stone and highly distinctive kinds of trellis, to more natural shapes like driftwood. Try painting metal poles in bright colours and fixing silver globes on top. You can even paint a dead tree that has been reduced to a few spare branches a strong colour, such as electric blue, to provide an extraordinary feature that will blend or contrast with the garden.

theatrical props

Even surprisingly everyday ornaments can be turned into wonderful, eye-catching features. Place a good-looking bench or urn at the end of a path or vista, and it immediately becomes a focal point. Once it takes on that role, dress it up and have fun. A statue can be given extra elegance by trailing a few stems of a small-leaved ivy around it, or frame it within a semi-circle of evergreen hedge or brightly coloured shrubs. Night-time lighting makes it even more potent and dramatic when it is one of the few parts of the garden being picked up by a spotlight.

Benches can be given extra prominence by siting them in a large space, where the lawn turns to gravel or paving, and the background planting, such as a clematis or climbing rose, is trained up a rustic fence. You can create a quiet, relaxing and beautiful place in the summer garden with careful planting.

left A floral arbour makes a rich decorative frame for a statue. The delicate shades of pink and purple roses, clematis and foxgloves make a pretty surround.

below Create a relaxing seating area by surrounding a bench with raised beds packed full of summer blooms.

containers

These are an excellent way of growing even more plants during the summer, in all kinds of surprising, unlikely places. Hanging baskets can be used beside outside doors, on sheds and pillars, and window boxes on walls at the end of the garden. Whenever you see a space on a wall, imagine it filled with containers packed with brightly coloured plants. The most sensational display is a bright white wall with 20 or 30 small pots, nailed up in rows. Plant them with pelargoniums, which come in all colours from soft salmon pink to brash red, or your favourite herbs.

above A hanging basket with trailing begonias in all its summer glory.

above right A terrace wall is ideal for pots full of bright pelargoniums.

below A pretty mix of purple lobelia and yellow *Bidens ferulifolia.*

tiered planting

If you have a small space, make the best use of it by packing in plants close together. Do it imaginatively, and the pots will be totally hidden by growth.

You can use all kinds of effects to create the tiers. Arrange pots on the top of a wall (firmly fixed in place) with more beneath, or nail up metal shelves. Try creating mobile herbaceous borders using dozens of pots on three platforms, 30cm (1ft), 60cm (2ft) and 90cm (3ft)

high, supported by bricks and strong boards. With over 200 plants you can transform a display into a mini tropical jungle. It will look stunning if you include plenty of lush foliage plants, along with occasional vivid flashes of red, pink, orange, yellow and white flowers.

foliage plants

Fun, unusual foliage plants that can be grown in pots include *Glaucium flavum* (yellow horned poppy), which has the most marvellous fleshy, blue-green, cabbage-like leaves, hairy stems, and 5cm (2in) wide yellow, poppy-like flowers that last a couple of days, followed by long seedheads.

The American *Darmera peltata* has dramatically veined, dark green leaves that grow 60cm (2ft) wide. *Ligularia stenocephala* 'The Rocket' has tall black flower stems and toothed leaves. And a rarely grown star is *Colutea* x *media*, which has blue-green foliage, and curving orange flowers, followed by translucent 8cm (3in) long pods.

window boxes

Inject lots of colour into a window box by cramming the plants close together. As long as you keep feeding them, the stress caused by overcrowding usually prompts them to flower prolifically. Try creating a lively summer display based on one dominant colour, such as blue, including different tones and hues, drawing the eye in to explore the subtle differences.

If you want strikingly contrasting schemes, use plenty of primary colours, with red and white, and blue and yellow, and a couple of trailing plants that lead the eye away, like the yellow *Bidens ferulifolia* with its prolific show of star-shaped flowers. If you have a courtyard, fill it with window boxes at different levels, which will help add colour at all heights.

above Blue petunias, blue brachycome daisies and *Convolvulus sabatius* offer similar hues and a lively mix.

left Mix flame reds and earthy-brown by planting up a terracotta window box with red zonal pelargoniums, red and yellow nasturtiums and red verbena.

distinctive displays

There are various ways of making sensational summer displays of pot plants. By grouping pots together you can create a big, dramatic show, with the containers largely hidden by the plants. Or use large, beautifully shaped containers, either standing alone or in small groups. Smaller, less eye-catching plants can produce wonderfully subtle effects in a group of attractive, rustically weathered pots. This kind of arrangement is particularly good for herbs.

star plants

Evergreen hebes have strong shapes and can easily be trimmed to keep them looking neat. They have spiky flowerheads in shades of blue, mauve, pink, red and white. Often the flowers fade as they age, so that the spikes are coloured at the ends and white lower down. Even better, there are plenty of small ones for pots, such as *Hebe* x *franciscana* 'Variegata', which has flashy yellow and green leaves and purple flowers. It grows 60cm (2ft) high and wide.

The South American cannas provide large, exotic, paddle-shaped leaves, and tall spikes of flowers that look like gladioli. Most have fresh green leaves, but those of 'Durban' are striped green and pink, while 'Wyoming' has leaves with a strong tinge of purple.

If you want to be even more exotic, try *Chamaerops humilis* (the bushy palm). In southern Europe, where it grows wild, it can grow 3m (10ft) high, but cramped in a pot, only half that. It has stiff, fan-shaped leaves in bluish grey-green. Though half-hardy, it will easily survive in a sheltered city garden.

above This weathered stone vase is a classic form suitable for placing on the ground or on a pedestal. Planted with bright red cannas and pelargoniums, it makes a bold statement.

right This pot has been painted with pink stripes to match the delicate pink and white flowers of this hebe.

top care tips

When planting your containers, make sure that you put plenty of drainage material in the base. Plastic foam chips or broken plant trays are effective and easy to come by. If the pot is light and liable to be blown over, it may be better to use heavy pebbles.

For plants that don't like dry conditions, a loam-based compost (soil mix) will dry out less quickly than the soilless types, and mixing in water-retaining gel will also help. A layer of shingle or large stones on the surface will reduce evaporation. It will also stop moss forming on the soil in wet weather, keep off slugs and snails, and set off the plants nicely.

You also need to give the plants a regular liquid feed in the summer because all the nutrients in the soil get washed out after about six weeks. Regular watering is crucial since roots cannot reach for reserves deep in the ground, and in sunny positions pots dry out extremely rapidly, so it is best to stick to drought-loving plants in these areas. If the roots curl out of the pot, either trim them back or move the plant into a larger container.

above left The choice of mellow terracotta pots, simply planted, set against the honey tones of the stone wall and gravel surface visually raises the temperature in this little courtyard.

above right Begonias will tolerate sunny conditions and make good planting companions for coleus and lampranthus.

left Nasturtiums associate well with tall, bold sunflowers in this large container.

garden schemes

The Victorians created better summer bedding schemes than anyone, with elaborate, ornate patterning in flowerbeds, using a wide variety of plants. And while it looks incredibly difficult, it is not. Try it on a small scale in a spare bed.

Start by drawing a plan, and keep it simple, with straight lines and rounded curves, avoiding tight angles and intricate shapes. Big and bold is best to begin with. Stick to four or five colours and plant up the design with annuals, making sure that you choose neat, uniform varieties that will not spoil the pattern as they grow.

free-flowing pathways

The arrangement of paths in the garden will have a big effect on the overall atmosphere – you can go for straight, clean geometric lines, or softly curving and winding ones.

above This watercourse is superbly laid out in a natural scheme, with an exciting range of flowers flourishing among the rocks.

right Different shades of *Impatiens*, busy Lizzie, are beautifully set off by silver-leaved plants in an elaborate, formal edging.

far right In this subtle informal scheme, arching, sword-like leaves are almost as important a feature as the bright blue agapanthus and orange crocosmia flowers.

right Metalwork arches clothed with pink and purple roses define a grass pathway bordered by blue veronica.

below A winding gravel path leads the eye down this narrow garden to a pretty octagonal summer house.

Paths can be made of decking, gravel, grass, pebbles, stone or frost-resistant bricks in a variety of patterns. Decking looks good but can be slippery in wet weather. Grass is sensational when mown on a bright day, but can get muddy in heavy rain. Gravel avoids both problems, always looks good, and can be covered with a top layer of more expensive coloured chippings or pebbles in different colours. Bricks or pavers laid in a herringbone pattern, for example, introduce a mellow warmth to the garden.

Grass paths are best among traditional cottage garden schemes, with arches of climbing roses or with fences and trailing climbers. To stop the grass growing into the beds, edge the paths with attractive terracotta 'rope' tiling.

above Complex garden designs can be created using versatile modern materials. Harsh lines can be softened using plants such as foxgloves and zantedeschias.

boxes often demand that they are arranged in straight, military lines. On a much larger scale you can try something like a flamboyant metal "sunshade", doubling as an aerial sculpture. It will mix with an adjoining show of traditional summer plants, and makes an elegant, architectural feature, which mushrooms out of the ground.

ethnic

An interesting alternative to the modern or rustic look, is adding ethnic shapes and colours. You can use authentic materials such as Moorish tiles, incorporate water features and large urns, or amalgamate your favourite ideas. Keep the design simple and use a mix of potted plants, lots of green foliage and a few flashes of bright colour. By lime-washing or painting walls white, a soft cream or completely beige, and creating a patterned pebble "patio", the whole area is transformed. You can also use small coloured tiles in raised ponds, grapes over a pergola, and rock gardens to add a touch of the Mediterranean. Make sure your choice of plants suits the style of decoration.

modern metal

Materials such as galvanized metal, zinc and stainless steel are being increasingly used in innovative, modern garden designs. They give a contemporary twist even to quite conventional planting schemes. They are ideal with modern architecture.

Raised metal beds and containers need stylish planting. Large succulents and cacti catch the eye, as do blue-grey cabbages, a range of flowering and aromatic herbs and even simple plantings of carnations (*Dianthus*). The hard square shapes of the

right Zinc containers are light enough for roof terraces and give a strikingly contemporary look to a garden.

opposite A backdrop of sunbleached shutters and a faded wall sets the Mediterranean atmosphere in this courtyard garden.

above A statue will always add interest, especially as a centrepiece in a pond.

above right Pots of busy Lizzies and pelargoniums make a vibrant surrounding for this lily pond.

right A gentle stream edged with rocks and subtle-coloured flowers provides a perfect setting for relaxing.

waterside gardens

There are many ways water can be used, from Islamic-style ponds in courtyards to mock hillside streams. The latter need pumps and pipes to keep the water circulating. Gardens with pronounced slopes are often hard to plant, but mock streams add a real flourish, and can be set off with rocks, pond plants, and architectural features right at the top emphasizing the sense of height. Use tall grasses to hide where the water runs into the pipe and to create the illusion that the stream runs away underground instead of being pumped back to the start.

On hot, dry, free-draining slopes grow drought-tolerant seaside or Mediterranean-style plants that can cope with long periods without water. With rich soil and sun, there will be plenty of suitable plants such as lavender, euphorbia, broom and cistus. However, you need not aim for the greatest possible variety, as in a typical garden scheme, but rather select a few colourful plants and let them ramble and roam and spread in a totally uncontrived way. It is back-to-nature gardening.

left In this seaside garden, the steep border has been landscaped with rocks and summer-flowering plants.

below A Mediterranean-style garden filled with lavender, cistus, euphorbia and asphodels reflects the luxuriance of sunny scrublands.

sweeping gardens

Larger rural gardens can be planted in natural ways. That means creating large swathes of plants that flower in the summer, much as they are found in the wild where they self-seed and spread unchecked. In this way, plants that may not look particularly exciting as individuals, and which are generally used as background elements, can often be as impressive as the more glamorous plants that usually get star billing.

Such a scheme can be successful with a minimum of maintenance if you match the plants to the conditions. In a damp, shady area, stick to plants that thrive in such a site. There is a surprisingly large choice.

SUMMER TASKS

The most important thing is to enjoy the garden during the summer. For a few months everything is madly flourishing, and the best way to keep the garden looking good is to make sure you do four things. Keep weeds under control, water young plants with short roots the moment they start to flag, mow the grass but never too severely, and look out for pests in the greenhouse, attacking any with biological controls. Hungry birds should pick off pests in the garden; see if that happens before using chemical sprays.

left Dramatic red hot pokers, purple globe thistles and dahlias make a bold, bright display.

right Deadhead lilacs as soon as they have finished flowering. Cut back to the first pair of leaves below the flowerhead.

plants at their best

- ❖ *Alchemilla mollis*
- ❖ *Allium*
- ❖ *Aquilegia*
- ❖ *Begonia*
- ❖ *Buddleja globosa*
- ❖ *Calendula*
- ❖ *Calluna vulgaris*
- ❖ *Cistus*
- ❖ *Cosmos*
- ❖ *Dianthus*
- ❖ *Digitalis*
- ❖ *Euphorbia*
- ❖ *Geranium*
- ❖ *Gladiolus*
- ❖ *Iris germanica* hybrids
- ❖ *Laburnum*
- ❖ *Lavandula*
- ❖ *Lupinus*
- ❖ *Nepeta* x *faassenii*
- ❖ *Paeonia*
- ❖ *Papaver orientale*
- ❖ *Philadelphus*
- ❖ *Rosa*
- ❖ *Tagetes*
- ❖ *Weigela*
- ❖ *Zantedeschia*

early summer

This is usually a busy time of year. The weather can be very variable, ranging from sudden late frosts, when you have to run out and cover tender plants, to the hottest day for nine months, when everything in the greenhouse bakes.

Early summer is also the period when any spring-sown seedlings should be putting on good growth and will need potting up or planting out in the garden. The weeds will be thriving as well as everything else, and it is vital that they are promptly removed before they take hold. Some are quick to flower, and if they are allowed to scatter their seed the problem will become much worse. Pests and diseases are also starting to thrive, and prompt action now will stop them from getting out of control, necessitating more drastic measures later. If you have a heavy rainfall early in the season, it is a good idea to apply a thick mulch to the flowerbeds, to help conserve moisture for the drier months ahead. A mulch also acts as an excellent soil conditioner.

Ironically, despite all the tasks that need doing, early summer can often be a disappointing time in the garden. The spring plants have finished, and the summer plants are not yet in their stride. If the garden looks a bit quiet and plain, it's only temporary and everything will be flourishing within a few weeks.

below Biological pest controls can be very successful if used properly.

below Thin seedlings, discarding the surplus ones, so that they do not become overcrowded.

above Keep hanging baskets, tubs and patio pots well watered, and they will reward you with ever more abundant flowers throughout the summer.

the greenhouse or conservatory

❖ Sow seed of biennial bedding plants, such as *Erysimum cheiri* (wallflowers), in seed trays for the next spring
❖ Feed pot plants regularly
❖ Take leaf cuttings of *Saintpaulia* (African violets) and *Streptocarpus*
❖ Start to feed tomatoes when the first truss of fruit has set
❖ If necessary, use biological pest control for greenhouse pests
❖ Pot up and pot on seedling pot plants as it becomes necessary
❖ Keep temperatures stable by using greenhouse shading, and increase ventilation
❖ Increase humidity by spraying water

the flower garden

❖ Give a thorough weed and apply a thick mulch, if not already done
❖ Sow daisy seed outdoors
❖ Sow hardy annuals
❖ Finish hardening off and planting tender plants
❖ Arrange containers for summer display
❖ Plant succulents for summer display
❖ Plant overwintered pelargoniums in beds and containers for summer display
❖ Plant chrysanthemums and marguerites in containers for summer display. Place in a bright, sheltered position
❖ Plant sunflower seedlings for late-summer display
❖ Pinch out shoots of chrysanthemums, marguerites and *Osteospermum* to encourage bushy plants
❖ Stake herbaceous plants
❖ Deadhead bedding plants regularly to ensure new buds develop
❖ Prune *Syringa* (lilac) and spiraea
❖ Watch out for signs of mildew and aphids on roses, and spray promptly if found

above If vine weevil grubs destroy your plants by eating the roots, try controlling them with a parasitic eelworm, which can be watered into the soil.

left Plant up a mixed window box with trailing and foliage plants. Arrange the plants before actually planting to judge the final effect you will achieve.

mid-summer

above To layer shrubs, bend down a stem in a shallow hole, peg it and cover with soil.

below Take semi-ripe cuttings of shrubs 5–10cm (2–4in) long. Choose shoots that are fully grown except for the soft tip. The base should be hardening.

Midsummer is a time for enjoying the results of your earlier efforts. There are always jobs to be done, of course, but you should also make time to relax. As most things are sown or planted, the emphasis is on weeding, watering and feeding. In dry summers water shortages can be a problem, but when you do water, do it thoroughly, as shallow watering will encourage surface rooting and make the plants even more vulnerable to drought.

Midsummer is a great time for assessing what looks good in the garden, and what could look even better. Take photographs and make notes, and start planning right now for next year's display. This is also a good time to move plants around. Always keep the rootball intact, and move it with as much of the soil as possible. If the roots do get severed, then cut back the top growth and remove the flowers to give the plant a good chance to recover. Water them in well and they should recover fairly quickly.

plants at their best

- ❖ Agapanthus
- ❖ Alcea
- ❖ Althaea
- ❖ Astilbe
- ❖ Begonia
- ❖ Calendula
- ❖ Cardiocrinum giganteum
- ❖ Cistus
- ❖ Clematis
- ❖ Cleome hassleriana
- ❖ Cosmos
- ❖ Digitalis
- ❖ Eryngium
- ❖ Gazania
- ❖ Geranium
- ❖ Gladiolus
- ❖ Hardy annuals
- ❖ Helianthemum
- ❖ Helianthus annuus
- ❖ Hydrangea
- ❖ Hypericum
- ❖ Jasminium officinale
- ❖ Kniphofia
- ❖ Lavandula
- ❖ Lilium
- ❖ Lonicera periclymenum
- ❖ Lupinus
- ❖ Monarda longifolia
- ❖ Nigella damascena
- ❖ Philadelphus 'Belle Etoile'
- ❖ Potentilla
- ❖ Rosa
- ❖ Summer bedding
- ❖ Verbascum
- ❖ Zantedeschia

above Carefully remove newly developing flower buds on your chrysanthemum plants to encourage larger flowers later in the season.

the greenhouse or conservatory

❖ Feed pot plants regularly
❖ Take semi-ripe cuttings of shrubs
❖ Feed tomatoes and chrysanthemums regularly
❖ Remove sideshoots and yellowing leaves from tomatoes regularly
❖ Keep a vigilant watch for pests and diseases
❖ Thin out the young fruit on grape vines
❖ Regularly check container plants and water twice a day if necessary
❖ Most tender plants should be outside now, where they benefit from the fresh air
❖ Thoroughly clean all pots that are no longer required, and store away
❖ Beware of high temperatures. Use shading and ventilation as necessary
❖ Spray water on the floor and benches to increase the humidity

above Divide flag irises by trimming the stumps to 5–8cm (2–3in) long. Replant the pieces of rhizome on a slight ridge of soil, covering the roots but leaving the tops exposed.

above To layer carnations, make a slit in a non-flowering shoot, below the lowest leaves. Peg the shoot into the soil.

the flower garden

❖ Apply a rose fertilizer once the main flush of flowering is over
❖ Feed greedy plants like geraniums and occasionally give a foliar feed
❖ Cut back lavender heads after flowering
❖ Deadhead bedding and border plants regularly to ensure new buds develop
❖ Hoe beds and borders regularly to keep down any weeds
❖ Divide and replant border irises
❖ Take semi-ripe cuttings
❖ Clip beech, holly, hornbeam and yew hedges towards the end of the period
❖ Layer shrubs and carnations
❖ Plant colchicums, to flower in the autumn, when they are available
❖ Transplant biennials and perennial seedlings to a nursery bed
❖ Order new bulb catalogues and bulbs for autumn delivery
❖ Disbud early-flowering chrysanthemums
❖ Mow the lawn except in very dry weather

above Use scissors, a sharp knife or secateurs to snip off dead flowerheads neatly and cleanly where they join the stem.

below Regularly pinch or cut out the sideshoots on cordon tomatoes.

above Plant prepared hyacinths for early flowering as soon as they are available.

late summer

This is usually a time of hot, dry weather, when there is a natural lull in the garden, and the efforts of spring and early summer sowing will have paid dividends. The chores of early autumn can wait until the holidays are over and cooler weather begins to return. Most of this month's work in the garden involves watering and routine maintenance like mowing and hoeing, and clipping hedges.

If you are tempted to leave any tender plants outside all winter, seeing if they will survive, then take some safety precautions. Snip off a few cuttings, and pot them up, tending them all winter just in case the parent gets killed. Constant soaking wet soil is as likely to kill the parent as freezing temperatures. Tackle the latter by adding a thick mulch.

plants at their best

- Agapanthus
- Alcea
- Begonia
- Buddleja davidii
- Canna
- Cardiocrinum giganteum
- Crocosmia
- Cosmos
- Erigeron
- Eucomis autumnalis 'White Dwarf'
- Fuchsia
- Hebe
- Helenium
- Hibiscus syriacus
- Hydrangea
- Hypericum
- Lavandula
- Lavatera
- Lilium
- Lobelia
- Lonicera periclymenum
- Monarda longifolia
- Passiflora caerulea
- Perovskia atriplicifolia
- Romneya
- Rosa
- Solidago

above Always label your cuttings. Keep the compost (soil mix) damp and pot up individually when well rooted. Protect them from frost.

the greenhouse or conservatory

- Pot up pelargoniums and overwinter indoors. Reduce the height of each plant by at least half and it will soon send out new shoots
- Pot up *Scaevola* and overwinter on an indoor windowsill or in a frost-free greenhouse. Cut plants right back
- Pot up *Gazania* and *Osteospermum* and overwinter in a frost-free, dry place for planting out in the spring
- Plant bulbs for a spring display
- Plant biennial bedding plants in containers for a spring display (raised from the seed sown last spring)
- Plant hyacinths for early flowering under glass
- Check cinerarias for leaf miners (white "tunnels" in the leaves). Remove the affected leaves or control with a systemic insecticide

above Fuchsias are really easy to root, and by taking cuttings now you will have young plants that can be overwintered. They will make good plants for next summer, or you can use them to provide more cuttings next spring.

above Take pelargonium cuttings now and overwinter the young plants in a light, frost-free place. Do not overwater, otherwise the cuttings will rot.

above This chrysanthemum is showing early signs of leaf miner damage. Often it may be possible to prevent spread if you act quickly and pinch off and destroy the first few affected leaves.

the flower garden

- ❖ Deadhead plants regularly
- ❖ Feed plants in containers frequently
- ❖ Hoe beds and borders to keep down weeds
- ❖ Take semi-ripe cuttings
- ❖ Clip beech, holly, hornbeam and yew hedges, and most evergreen hedges, if not already done
- ❖ Plant colchicums to flower in the autumn
- ❖ Trim flower stems of perennial plants like *Dianthus* (carnations)
- ❖ Plant bulbs for autumn display
- ❖ Start planting spring-flowering bulbs
- ❖ Take fuchsia and pelargonium cuttings
- ❖ Start sowing hardy annuals to overwinter (only in mild areas or if you provide winter protection)
- ❖ Prune rambler roses
- ❖ Layer border carnations
- ❖ Mow the lawn except in very dry weather
- ❖ Water the lawn in dry spells, but a few good soaks will be better than many sprinklings that do not penetrate deeply
- ❖ Watch out for pests and diseases on roses and other vulnerable plants
- ❖ Feed and disbud dahlias as necessary
- ❖ Transplant polyanthus seedlings into their flowering positions in beds and borders

above Chrysanthemums and dahlias benefit from regular feeding. Use a quick-acting general fertilizer or a high-potash feed, but do not boost with too much nitrogen.

left Provided you can keep your greenhouse frost-free during the winter – ideally at a minimum of 7°C (45°F) – it is worth sowing plants to bloom next spring.

the autumn garden

CREATING AN AUTUMN GARDEN

You can pack plenty of bright vivid colours into the autumn garden. There are dozens of plants at their peak now, and the whole show can be set off by the even more spectacular "bonfire" of leaf colours as scores of deciduous trees and shrubs flare up red and orange and golden yellow. While it is tempting to think that the autumn garden should bow out gracefully with beautiful pale-coloured seedheads, which it can easily do with the right choice of plants, it can also end on a wonderful high with bold colours and brilliant displays.

left Many grasses are at their best in the autumn. The flowering spikelets turn beige and silvery and look attractive in the autumn sun.

right A smart autumn combination is richly coloured *Crocosmia* 'Lucifer' and golden brown *Helenium* 'Waldtraut'.

THE KEY TO A LIVELY, RICHLY COLOURED AUTUMN garden is to make sure that it has a first-rate selection of bulbs, perennials, grasses, conifers, and, best of all, shrubs and trees that come into their own during this period. Those with an end of season "flare up" offer a rich array of purple and scarlet, with lashings of yellow and orange.

gumballs, maples and burnt sugar

The best way to find the most colourful autumn plants is to visit private and public gardens which have a superb autumn show. Identify the best plants, working in layers down from the trees to the ground. A liquidambar tree, like a flaming brand at 6m (20ft) high, might be far too big for most gardens but there is usually a lively alternative. *Liquidambar styraciflua* 'Gumball' has just as many colours but is a sensational shrubby mound, at just 2m (6ft) high.

below *Sedum spectabile* provides a welcome burst of bright colour in the autumn garden. It attracts bees and butterflies, and livens up the front of a border.

Cultivars of the the Japanese maples (*Acer palmatum*) can be anything from 75cm (2½ft) to 8m (25ft) high and have a fantastic range of deep colours. One of the best for a medium-size garden is the slow-growing 'Crimson Queen', whose leaves turn reddish-purple, and it never exceeds 75cm (2½ft). If a maple does start getting too big for the garden, it can always be pruned to size. They look best when half the richly coloured leaves are still hanging on, giving views through bare branches to the rest of the garden, and half are lying like a radiant rug on the ground.

left *Acer palmatum* produces a brilliant display of scarlet leaves.

below The soft beige tones of *Cortaderia* blend in well with bolder autumnal colours.

Cercidiphyllum japonicum (katsura tree) is the autumn tree with a big difference because, as well as flamboyant colours, it has the terrific scent of burnt sugar and toffee apples. As the leaves start to fall they release a wonderful scent in a wide radius, up to 30m (100ft) away. The katsura tree needs to be given plenty of space to grow, because it can reach 6m (20ft) high after 20 years; if space really is quite restricted, prune it to one trunk because it often produces several stems.

grasses and perennials

The countryside in autumn is largely beige and brown as grasses start to fade, and the leaves of many trees start to crinkle, die and fall. Gardens need plenty of these colours as they inject a traditional low-key feel to the end of the year. They provide an essential link between the brighter summer colours and winter.

Some grasses, like pampas grass, have much more style though. *Cortaderia selloana* has gigantic late summer and early autumn feathery plumes. Most of the grasses can be left standing right through the autumn and winter before being cut back to be replaced by fresh new growth early the following spring. By leaving them unpruned, you will ensure that the garden has plenty of stems and seedheads to keep it architecturally alive right through the dormant season.

Other perennials will need cutting back at the end of autumn. *Sedum spectabile* (ice plant) flowers at the end of summer into early autumn, adding pink flowers which bring the autumn show of colours right down to the ground. With a wide, imaginative planting of bulbs such as colchicums, nerines and sternbergias, you can guarantee a richly coloured garden, in all hues, from the evergreens to loud bursts of magenta red with patches of soft and gentle beige.

AUTUMN PLANTS

The following pages provide a selection of the best autumn plants. They include bulbs, perennials, grasses, shrubs, climbers, trees and conifers. Start by planting a few in each category and then, over the following years, begin filling in the gaps, creating some powerful eye-catching autumn colours in different areas of the garden, and more low-key, gentler colours in other parts. Look to see which plants thrive best in the conditions in your garden, and you can gradually build up a beautiful autumn display.

left Rudbeckias provide some of the brightest autumn colours with their vivid yellow flowers. Most have a distinctive central disc. Easy to grow, they thrive in a hot, sunny position.

bulbs

There is a small select group of highly desirable bulbs for the end of the year. They provide a beautiful contrast to the more brazen shows of colour on the trees and shrubs, and help keep the eye moving around the garden. Most require well-drained soil and plenty of sun in order to thrive, though there are some that prefer shady, moist conditions. Do not remove the foliage until it has turned brown, or next year's display will suffer.

Canna

Commonly known as Indian shot plants, or Indian reed flowers, these are exotic plants for the autumn garden. Even if they did not flower, they would be worth growing for their large, smooth leaves. Use them with grasses and brilliant dahlias to bring the season to a close with a flourish. Stictly speaking they are rhizomatous perennials, but they are planted like bulbs. They are excellent in large containers.

C. hybrids

The cannas grown in gardens are hybrids, of which there are many. All the following have green leaves unless otherwise indicated. All are half-hardy. 'Black Knight' has dark red flowers and bronze leaves. 'Brandywine' has scarlet red-orange flowers. 'City of Portland' has yellow-edged, rose pink flowers. 'Ingeborg' has salmon pink flowers and bronze leaves. The free-flowering 'Lucifer' has yellow-edged crimson flowers. 'Orchid' has pink flowers. 'President' has bright red flowers. The flowers of 'Primrose Yellow' are pale yellow. 'Richard Wallace' has canary yellow flowers. 'Rosemond Coles' has yellow-edged, bright red flowers. The orange flowers of 'Wyoming' are frilled and have darker orange edges; the leaves are bronze. Smaller cannas can be planted together in groups, but do not overcrowd them and allow room for their leaves to develop. The taller cannas can be used as individual specimens, providing the focal point of a bright display.
Flowering height To 2m (6ft)
Flowering time Midsummer to early autumn
Hardiness Half-hardy

below left *Canna* 'Brandywine'.

below right Many canna hybrids have dramatically coloured leaves, such as *C.* 'Assaut', which are deep purple.

opposite left *Colchicum speciosum* 'Album'.

opposite right *Colchicum speciosum*.

Colchicum

These pretty bulbs are often known as autumn crocus, or naked ladies (or naked boys in the United States). The flowers of colchicums are always a surprise when they appear, and it is easy to forget that the corms are in the garden. The leaves, large and glossy, do not appear until the following spring (the best time to transplant them, if this is necessary). They are excellent in light woodland or planted around shrubs. In borders the leaves can be a nuisance in the spring. Robust types are also excellent for naturalizing in grass. *C. speciosum* is the most widely grown member of the genus, and produces goblet-shaped, pink flowers in autumn. 'Album' has 1 to 3 goblet-shaped, weather-resistant, white flowers that are green at the base. It is a good plant in open ground in borders or grassland. *C.* 'The Giant' is one of many hybrids, with large, lilac-pink flowers. Plant them in light shade, for example beneath deciduous trees and on the sunny side of shrubs.

Flowering height To 15cm (6in)
Flowering time Autumn
Hardiness Mostly fully hardy

Crocosmia

These colourful perennials are originally from South Africa. Excellent as they are as border plants, combining well with roses and annuals, they also look effective when grown in isolation in large groups. The leaves are linear, lance-shaped, mainly ribbed and about 60–100cm (2–3ft) long. The flowers are excellent for cutting. *C.* x *crocosmiiflora* (montbretia) is a hybrid group including many garden-worthy forms. They can be grown just about anywhere in the garden, provided they are given sun or light shade, and fertile soil. They can be used to arch over the edge of a pond, their reflections caught in the water, to soften the edge of a straight path, and to provide a colourful contrast next to an evergreen shrub. The key to a good show is a bold group of corms clustered close together so that they have plenty of impact. 'Emily McKenzie' has orange flowers with brown throats from late summer to autumn. Also flowering from late summer to autumn, 'Solfatare' produces a succession of apricot-yellow flowers among its grassy, bronze-tinged leaves. 'Jackanapes' has tri-coloured, orange, red and yellow flowers.
Flowering height To 1.5m (5ft)
Flowering time Late summer to autumn
Hardiness Fully hardy

Cyclamen

The genus includes 19 species of tuberous perennials, found in a wide variety of habitats from the eastern Mediterranean to North Africa and the Middle East. The rounded to heart-shaped leaves often have attractive silver markings. They like well-drained, humus-rich soil in sun or partial shade.

C. hederifolium

This species was formerly known as *C. neapolitanum*. The pink flowers have a darker red stain towards the mouth. The pretty ivy- or heart-shaped leaves are often patterned. *C. mirabile* has pale pink flowers with serrated petals and purple-stained mouths. The leaves are heart-shaped and patterned with silver blotches.
Flowering height 10cm (4in)
Flowering time Autumn
Hardiness Fully hardy

Nerine

This is a genus of about 30 species of bulbs found on well-drained mountainous sites in Africa. The common name, Guernsey lily, is properly applied to *N. sarniensis*. The flowers appear in the autumn, followed by the leaves in late winter, and the plant goes dormant in summer, when it likes a dry, warm period. They

flower best when the bulbs are packed quite close together. *N. bowdenii* has umbels of up to 7 or more funnel-shaped, slightly scented, pink flowers, each to 7.5cm (3in) across, with wavy-edged, recurved petals, borne on stout stems. It must have a well-drained site and is a good choice for the foot of a sunny wall, where the pink flowers look striking. In cold areas, provide a dry mulch in winter.

Flowering height 45cm (18in)
Flowering time Autumn
Hardiness Fully hardy

Sternbergia

This genus of 8 species of dwarf bulb is found on hillsides, scrub and pine forests in southern Europe, Turkey and central Asia. They are similar to crocuses but have 6, not 3, stamens and grow from bulbs rather than corms. Like the crocus, some species are autumn-flowering, and some flower in spring. All parts are poisonous. They need hot sun and well-drained soil that dries out in summer. *S. lutea* has yellow, goblet-shaped flowers, 4cm (1½in) across, that appear at the same time as the dark green, strap-like leaves.

Flowering height 15cm (6in)
Flowering time Autumn
Hardiness Frost hardy

perennials

Just when most summer perennials are well past their best, and getting ready for the dormant season, a few others are actually about to peak. The following, especially the asters, provide some of the best plants for the garden at any time of the year, let alone the autumn. They add a bright range of colours and shades, giving the border a much needed end-of-season lift.

Aster

This large genus includes the well-known Michaelmas daisies, essential plants for the autumn garden, many of which flower from late summer until the first frosts. Most also last well as cut flowers. The species are as worthy of consideration as the hybrids, some of which have an annoying tendency towards mildew (although all those described are trouble-free). The genus also includes annuals. Asters will grow in any reasonably fertile soil, in sun or light shade. Some will do well in poor soil. The taller forms often benefit from staking, especially in sites where they are exposed to strong wind, which can easily spoil them.

below *Aster turbellinus.*

A. ericoides

The species, which is native to North America, has given rise to several garden-worthy forms. They have wiry stems that are starred with flowers, all with yellow centres, in autumn. 'Blue Star' has pale blue flowers; 'Golden Spray' has white flowers; 'Pink Cloud' has light mauve-pink flowers.
Flowering height 75cm (30in)
Flowering time Late summer to late autumn
Hardiness Fully hardy

A. x frikartii

This group of vigorous hybrids includes some of the best of the Michaelmas daisies, all with a long flowering season. 'Mönch' is an outstanding selection, which has large, lavender-blue flowers carried freely on branching stems. It is an excellent companion to shrubby lavateras. 'Wonder of Stafa' usually needs staking and has pinkish-blue flowers.
Flowering height 75cm (30in)
Flowering time Late summer to early autumn
Hardiness Fully hardy

A. laterifolius

The species has an unusual habit: the erect stems produce flowering sideshoots, almost at right angles, giving a tiered effect. The flowers are white to pale lilac. 'Horizontalis', which is rather more spreading, has pale lilac flowers. The coppery tinges acquired by its dainty leaves as the weather turns colder enhance the appeal of the plant.
Flowering height 90cm (3ft)
Flowering time Midsummer to mid-autumn
Hardiness Fully hardy

A. novi-belgii

Although generally applied to the whole genus, strictly the common name, Michaelmas daisy, belongs to this species alone, the parent of a bewildering number of garden forms. It is often found growing as a weed, brightening up railway cuttings and areas of rough land with its violet-blue flowers in early autumn, which suggests a use in a wild garden or grass. The colours of the garden forms range from white, through all shades of pink, to pale and dark lavender-blue and some purples. They vary in height from dwarf forms, which are good at the edge of a border, to more substantial plants. One of the best of the taller varieties is 'Climax', which has pale lavender-blue flowers in early autumn. Among the good dwarf forms are 'Jenny', which has purplish-red flowers, and 'Lady in Blue', which has lavender-blue flowers.

Flowering height 30cm–1.5m (1–5ft)
Flowering time Late summer to mid-autumn
Hardiness Fully hardy

A. turbinellus

A refined-looking species from the United States, this has wiry stems that carry violet-blue daisies in autumn.

Flowering height To 1.2m (4ft)
Flowering time Early to mid-autumn
Hardiness Fully hardy

Helenium

These valuable daisy-like flowers are easily grown and merit a place in any border planned for autumn interest. Together with dahlias and chrysanthemums, they bring a warm glow to the garden at the end of the season, and they look good with a range of grasses. The following hybrids all flower from late summer to mid-autumn. 'Indianersommer' has rich golden-yellow flowers; 'Moerheim Beauty', one of the best known, has rich brownish-red flowers that age lighter brown; 'The Bishop' has yellow flowers with dark eyes.

Flowering height To 1.5m (5ft)
Flowering time Midsummer to autumn
Hardiness Fully hardy

Physalis alkekengi

Commonly known as the Chinese lantern, this is a good plant in the cottage garden. The orange, papery shells surrounding the fruit are excellent for use in dried arrangements. During winter the shells slowly disintegrate, leaving only the veins and exposing the fruit within a wiry skeleton cage. Plant in well-drained soil, in full sun. *P. peruviana* is known as Cape gooseberry.

Flowering height To 2m (6ft)
Flowering time Midsummer (late summer to autumn seedheads)
Hardiness Fully hardy

above *Aster novi-belgii* 'Peace'.

below left to right
Helenium 'Indianersommer', *Physalis alkekengi* and *Helenium* 'Waldtraut' with *Crocosmia* 'Lucifer'.

above *Rudbeckia fulgida.*

Rudbeckia

Coneflowers are easy to grow, sturdy and essential plants for borders in early autumn. The petals of the daisy-like flowers droop away from the contrasting centres in an appealing way. They combine well with grasses. *R. fulgida*, or black-eyed Susan, is an excellent garden plant. *R. fulgida* var. *sullivantii* 'Goldsturm' has large, richer yellow flowerheads. *R.* 'Goldquelle' has double flowers with yellow petals and greenish centres.
Flowering height To 2m (6ft)
Flowering time Late summer to autumn
Hardiness Fully hardy

Schizostylis

Kaffir lilies will brighten up the autumn and early winter garden with their elegant spikes of fresh-looking flowers. Since they spread rapidly, regular division is advisable. There are a number of desirable selections. *S. coccinea* looks like a small gladiolus, with slender, grassy leaves and spikes of cup-shaped, red flowers. Among the many cultivars are 'Major' (syn. 'Grandiflora'), which has bright clear red flowers; 'Sunrise' (syn. 'Sunset'), with salmon pink flowers; and 'Viscountess Byng', one of the last to flower, with pale pink flowers.
Flowering height 60cm (2ft)
Flowering time Late summer to early winter
Hardiness Frost hardy

Sedum

These reliable plants have broad heads of sweetly-scented pink to mauve flowers that attract bees and butterflies. They need a sunny site, and their fleshy leaves enable them to tolerate drought. The genus also includes small species for the rock garden.

S. 'Herbstfreude'

This robust hybrid is the best-known of all sedums. It has large, fleshy grey-green leaves and heads of scented flowers in the autumn, deep pink at first, turning to salmon-pink and aging to a dramatic, rich brick-red.
Flowering height 60cm (2ft)
Flowering time Early autumn
Hardiness Fully hardy

S. spectabile

Probably one of the parents of 'Herbstfreude', this species is commonly known as the ice plant. It is roughly similar to the hybrid but is smaller and has pinkish-mauve flowers. Among the many cultivars are *S. s.* 'Iceberg', which is a good white. *S. s.* 'Brilliant' produces an abundance of bright rose-pink flowers from late summer to autumn.
Flowering height 45cm (18in)
Flowering time Late summer to early autumn
Hardiness Fully hardy

right *Sedum* 'Herbstfreude'.

far right *Sedum spectabile.*

Zauschneria

Often called Californian fuchsia, this genus of sun-loving perennials provides brilliant material for the front of a border, the funnel-shaped flowers being a vivid scarlet in most cases. They are best with the shelter of a warm wall in cold areas, where they are not reliably hardy. They also thrive and look spectacular when growing on the sunny side of a dry stone wall. Their key requirement is excellent drainage.

They can be grown in gravel gardens, especially in areas with low rainfall. *Z. californica* is the best-known species, and has attractive, lance-shaped, grey-green leaves, the perfect foil to the luminous scarlet flowers, produced from late summer to early autumn. 'Dublin' has slightly longer, bright orange-red flowers.

Flowering height To 30cm (12in)
Flowering time Late summer to early autumn
Hardiness Frost hardy

above, clockwise from top left *Schizostylis coccinea, Sedum spectabile* 'Iceberg', *Zauschneria californica, Sedum spectabile.*

above *Cortaderia selloana albolineata.*

below *Stipa gigantea.*

right top to bottom *Hordeum jubatum, Molinia caerulea.*

grasses

Ornamental grasses are excellent for providing shape and structure throughout autumn and winter – the flowering heads can be left standing until spring. Some are imposing plants that make impressive specimens, give height to borders or provide accents, while others can create soft, feathery drifts to soften any colour scheme. Some bamboos make good screens, as well as providing useful stakes. All the grasses described, unless otherwise indicated, like a well-drained site in full sun.

Cortaderia

Commonly known as pampas grass, there are about 24 species of evergreen, tussock-forming grasses in the genus. Their coloured, glistening plumes can be a decorative feature in autumn or winter when covered with frost. Always wear gloves and take care when cutting back the plants in spring: the leaves are lethally sharp. *C. selloana* 'Sunningdale Silver' is an outstanding form, with plumes of silver-cream flowers in late summer and autumn.

Flowering height 3m (10ft)
Flowering time Late summer to early autumn
Hardiness Mostly fully hardy

Hordeum

Commonly known as barley, the genus contains 20 species of annuals and perennials, including *H. vulgare*, the well-known cereal crop, which are mainly of interest to the gardener because of their flowers. They are splendid additions to late summer and autumn borders, combining well with dahlias and Michaelmas daisies. *H. jubatum* (foxtail barley or squirrel-tail barley), from north-eastern Asia and North America, is an attractive annual grass. The showy plumes of straw-coloured flowers appear in late summer and early autumn, making this excellent for filling gaps in borders towards the end of the season.

Flowering height 50cm (20in)
Flowering time Late summer to early autumn
Hardiness Fully hardy

Miscanthus

These elegant perennial grasses are handsome enough to serve as specimens, besides their other uses in beds and borders and for cutting. They develop pleasing russet tints in the autumn. *M. sinensis* is a clump-forming species from eastern Asia with bluish-green leaves and pale grey spikelets, tinged with purple, in the autumn. 'Gracillimus' (maiden grass) is tall, with narrow leaves, which curl at the tips, and plumes of buff-yellow flowers in the autumn. One of the most attractive selections is 'Kleine Fontäne', which produces upright clumps of leaves and heads of pale pink flowers.
Flowering height To 2.4m (8ft)
Flowering time Late summer to autumn
Hardiness Fully hardy

Molinia

These are graceful perennial grasses that look delightful in herbaceous and mixed borders. They like moist but well-drained soil, preferably acid, in sun or partial shade. *M. caerulea* (purple moor grass) is a species from Europe and south-western Asia and has green foliage that turns yellow in the autumn. Upright stems are topped with purplish flowerheads from late summer to autumn. *M. caerulea* subsp. *caerulea* 'Variegata' is an elegant form, with green and white striped leaves, which are sometimes tinged pink, and loose purple-grey flowers on arching stems in late summer and autumn.
Flowering height To 1.5m (5ft)
Flowering time Spring to autumn
Hardiness Fully hardy

Phyllostachys

The 80 or so evergreen bamboos in the genus are elegant enough for use as specimens in large gardens, or at the back of large borders as a backdrop to other plants. They like moist but well-drained soil in full sun or partial shade. Mature specimens of the imposing *P. bambusoides* (giant timber bamboo) have thick green canes that can be used for building. It has copious, broad, glossy, dark green leaves. *P. b.* 'Allgold' (syn. 'Holochrysa', 'Sulphurea') has golden-yellow canes, sometimes striped with green. *P. nigra* (black bamboo) is a Chinese species with canes that become black with age, a good contrast to the abundant green leaves.
Height To 7.5m (25ft)
Hardiness Fully hardy

Stipa

Commonly known as feather or needle grass, these are lovely grasses that make fine border plants. *S. arundinacea* (pheasant's tail grass) is an excellent grass for the autumn garden, a New Zealand species with long, tawny-beige foliage that intensifies in colour as the temperature drops. Thin stems carry brownish flowers in late summer. *S. calamagrostis* is good for planting in drifts. With its narrow, arching leaves, it blends happily with a range of plants. The silky flowerheads, which appear in summer, are initially green with a reddish tinge, fading to golden-yellow in late summer.
Flowering height 1m (3ft)
Flowering time Summer to autumn
Hardiness Fully hardy

above *Stipa calamagrostis.*

below left *Miscanthus.*

below *Phyllostachys bambusoides* 'Castilloni'.

shrubs

Many shrubs produce a wonderful display of autumn foliage or an eye-catching show of berries. Hungry birds might strip the branches of berries quite quickly, but with luck many will hang on through winter. Other shrubs look good when they have been topiarized and some can even be pruned so that they have striking bare legs with all the attractive leafy growth at the top.

Abelia

These evergreens are greatly valued for their graceful habit and late flowers, which last from midsummer to late autumn. They like well-drained soil in full sun, preferably against a wall in cold areas. *A.* x *grandiflora* is of garden origin and has slightly scented, white flowers from midsummer to autumn. 'Gold Spot' (syn. 'Aurea', 'Gold Strike', 'Goldsport') has greenish-yellow leaves.

below left to right
Abelia x *grandiflora, Berberis temolaica* and *Abelia* x *grandiflora* 'Gold Spot'.

Height To 2m (6ft)
Flowering time Summer and autumn
Hardiness Frost hardy

Abutilon

These elegant shrubs produce appealing lampshade-like flowers from late summer into autumn. They are sometimes trained as standards and used as dot plants in park bedding schemes. They are also good in containers, either on their own or as a central feature in a mixed planting. They need a well-drained site in full sun. *A. megapotanicum*, a trailing abutilon, is an evergreen or semi-evergreen species with orange-red and yellow, lantern-like flowers and maple-like leaves. The leaves of *A. m.* 'Variegatum' are mottled with yellow. This makes a good standard.
Height To 5m (16ft)
Flowering time Late summer to autumn
Hardiness Half or frost hardy

Berberis

An important genus, barberry is tough and hardy, and includes both evergreens and deciduous species, all with spiny stems. Although some are almost too familiar as hedging, there are also some very choice species that are well worth seeking out. The forms with coloured leaves make excellent specimens, but

beware of the sharp spines. They like well-drained soil and can tolerate partial shade, but produce better autumn colour and berries in full sun. Overgrown and straggly plants can be cut back in spring.

B. temolaica

A very handsome deciduous berberis, this slow-growing plant is difficult to propagate but is well worth looking out for. It has glaucous green leaves on whitened stems, lemon-yellow spring flowers and egg-shaped, crimson autumn fruits. Plants can be cut back hard annually or every two years for the interest of the winter stems.

Height 1.5m (5ft)
Flowering time Late spring (autumn berries)
Hardiness Fully hardy

B. thunbergii

This variable deciduous shrub has a number of interesting selections, all of which do best in fertile soil. The purple leaves of *B. thunbergii* f. *atropurpurea* turn orange in autumn. 'Aurea' has soft yellow leaves and is best in some shade. 'Helmond Pillar' is a distinctive upright selection with dark purple-red leaves. The popular and distinctive 'Rose Glow' has purple leaves swirled with pink and cream turning lipstick red in autumn. On 'Silver Beauty', the leaves are mottled with creamy white.

Height To 1.5m (5ft)
Flowering time Mid-spring (summer and autumn berries)
Hardiness Fully hardy

Calluna vulgaris

There are many excellent kinds of heather, which are often best used in groups to make a tapestry of colours and undulating shapes. They like an open site in full sun, with well-drained, humus-rich, acid soil. 'Arran Gold' has purple flowers and bright golden-yellow foliage, which turns lime green flecked with red in winter. 'Dark Beauty' has blood-red flowers and dark green foliage. 'Darkness' has deep crimson-pink flowers and mid-green foliage.

Height To 60cm (2ft)
Flowering time Midsummer to late autumn
Hardiness Fully hardy

above left to right *Berberis thunbergii* f. *atropurpurea*, *Abutilon megapotanicum* 'Variegatum' and *Calluna vulgaris* 'Arran Gold'.

below *Calluna vulgaris* 'Darkness'.

above left to right
Cotinus coggygria 'Royal Purple', *Cotoneaster lacteus* 'Heaselands Coral' and *Enkianthus perulatus.*

below Smoke bush.

Cotinus

Commonly called smoke bush, there are two species of impressive deciduous shrubs in the genus. The purple-leaved forms have spectacular autumn colour. They make large, rangy shrubs, but can be cut back hard for larger leaves, albeit at the expense of the flowers. The flowers are tiny, but carried in large panicles, looking like smoke from a distance – hence the common name. They are produced reliably only in hot summers. In cold areas it is better to cut the plant back hard annually for an improved foliage display. The purple-leaved forms are indispensable in a red or purple border. *C. coggygria* is the plain green species. Far better known is the selection 'Royal Purple', grown principally for its coin-like, dramatic purple leaves, which turn vivid red in the autumn. *C.* 'Grace' is similar to *C. coggygria* 'Royal Purple', but is larger and has oval leaves, which turn dark brownish-red in the autumn.
Height To 5m (16ft)
Flowering time Midsummer (autumn foliage)
Hardiness Fully hardy

Cotoneaster

This is an important shrub genus, containing both evergreen and deciduous species. Cotoneasters are tough, hardy, tolerant plants, which make excellent foils to a huge range of other showier plants. There are scores of different cotoneasters, in all sizes from 30cm (12in) to large shrubs and trees. Bees appreciate their creamy-white flowers in early summer, and birds enjoy their autumn berries. *C. dammeri*, an evergreen or semi-evergreen species, is an outstanding ground cover plant, carpeting the ground and thriving in many difficult garden situations. The plant flowers in early summer and bears scarlet berries in autumn. *C. frigidus* 'Cornubia' is a tree-like shrub, bearing bright red fruit in autumn, which is good enough to use as a specimen in a small garden. *C. horizontalis* is a versatile deciduous species, which can be grown as a wall shrub (or even up a tree trunk) or allowed to cascade over a bank, both of which methods display its unusual 'herringbone' habit. It has excellent autumn leaf colour, along with an impressive display of vivid red berries. *C. lacteus* is a dense shrub with an abundant crop of early summer flowers followed by orange-red berries. It is excellent hedging material.
Height To 3m (10ft)
Flowering time Spring to summer (autumn berries)
Hardiness Fully hardy

Enkianthus perulatus

Grow this plant for the small white flowers which appear in the spring, but better still, the superb flame red autumn foliage. It likes moist, well-drained, humus-rich soil, preferably acid, in sun or partial shade.
Height To 2m (6ft)
Flowering time Mid-spring (autumn foliage)
Hardiness Fully hardy

Erica

Also known as heathers, these are the familiar heaths, scrubby plants that can be used to carpet large tracts of land. They form the largest genus of heaths (the other two are *Calluna* and *Daboecia*), with some 700 or more evergreen species, and are particularly valued in the autumn and winter garden, although there are species that flower at other times of year. In smaller gardens, ericas are excellent in island beds, either on their own (or with *Calluna* and *Daboecia*) or with dwarf conifers, with which they associate happily. They are also ideal container plants. Most types of heather need acid soil, but unlike most of the summer-flowering heathers, those described here will tolerate alkaline soil.

E. carnea

Alpine or winter heath. This is an important species of carpeting heaths. The flowering season is from late autumn to mid-spring, with plants in milder climates being as much as two months earlier than those in colder areas. Generally they are in flower for six to eight weeks. They like well-drained soil in sun or partial shade. The following selections of cultivars are all hardy. 'Aurea' has pink flowers and gold foliage tipped with orange in spring. 'Fiddler's Gold' has bronze foliage and pink flowers. 'Golden Starlet' has white flowers and glowing yellow foliage, which turns lime green in winter. 'Myretoun Ruby' (syn. 'Myreton Ruby') has pink flowers, which turn magenta then crimson, and dark green foliage. 'Rosy Gem' has lilac-pink flowers and dark green foliage. The vigorous 'Springwood White' has white flowers. 'Westwood Yellow' has shell-pink flowers initially that darken to lilac-pink, and yellow foliage throughout the year.

Height 15cm (6in)
Flowering time Late autumn to spring
Hardiness Fully hardy

E. vagans

Cornish heath or wandering heath. A vigorous, evergreen, bushy species that provides flowers in autumn (some selections coming into flower in late summer). Regular pruning after flowering will keep plants neat, though the faded flowers, if left on the plant, will turn an attractive russet brown in winter. 'Kervensis Alba' has white flowers. 'Summertime' has shell-pink flowers. 'Valerie Proudley' has sparse, white flowers and bright lemon-yellow foliage.

Height To 80cm (32in)
Flowering time Midsummer to mid-autumn
Hardiness Fully hardy

below left to right *Erica vagans* 'Valerie Proudley', *E. carnea* 'Rosy Gem' and *E. c.* 'Fiddler's Gold'.

above Bright red leaves of *Euonymus alatus.*

below left to right
Euonymus with bright red berries, *E. fortunei* 'Emerald 'n' Gold' and the deep pink berries of *Gaultheria angustifolia.*

Euonymus

Commonly known as a spindle tree, the genus includes about 175 species of deciduous, semi-evergreen and evergreen shrubs, trees and climbers. The evergreen shrubs make excellent ground cover and some can even climb walls. Deciduous types have both spectacular autumn leaf colour and showy fruits. They like well-drained soil in full sun or light shade; evergreen shrubs need protection from cold winds.

E. alatus

A deciduous shrub with distinguishing bluish-purple autumn fruits. They split to reveal bright orange seeds at the same time as the leaves redden, but persist on the branches for a while after the leaves have fallen. It is suitable for a wild garden or in a hedgerow-type planting and will ultimately make a fine specimen.
Height 2m (6ft)
Flowering time Early summer (autumn foliage)
Hardiness Fully hardy

E. fortunei

This evergreen is exclusively grown in its variegated forms, of which there are a great many. The following are all hardy. 'Emerald 'n' Gold' has leaves edged yellow. 'Harlequin' is a dwarf plant, with mottled white and green leaves, useful as ground cover if planted in groups. Most handsome of all is 'Silver Queen', which has leaves broadly edged with creamy white. It is slow-growing but worthwhile and spectacular as a climber, more if wall-trained.
Height 90cm (3ft)
Flowering time Early summer (autumn foliage)
Hardiness Fully hardy

Gaultheria

There are about 170 species of these evergreen shrubs with alternate, quite leathery leaves and small bell- or urn-shaped flowers. In the autumn they produce quite large, spherical berries. They can be planted in heather and rock gardens, and are also suitable for woodland gardens. They need moist, peaty, acid soil in partial shade. The fruits are edible, but other parts of the plant can cause mild stomach upsets. *G. mucronata* (syn. *Pernettya mucronata*) is a compact shrub. It produces nodding white, or sometimes pink-flushed, flowers in late spring to summer. In autumn, fruits or berries appear, in various shades from white to purple-red.
Height To 1.2m (4ft)
Flowering time Early summer (autumn berries)
Hardiness Mostly fully hardy

Photinia

These excellent shrubs are grown mainly for the brilliance of their spring foliage. They suit a mixed or shrub border and make a good alternative to pieris in gardens with alkaline soil. *P. davidiana* is a handsome shrub, semi-evergreen in all but the coldest areas. Its long-lasting crimson berries ripen in autumn. Some of the leaves turn bright red at the same time, while others remain green. *P.* x *fraseri* is a hybrid group including many excellent selected forms. The new growth of the spreading form 'Birmingham' is deep coppery red. 'Red Robin' has spectacular bright red young stems and leaves in vivid contrast to the glossy green older leaves.

Height 3m (10ft)

Flowering time Spring and summer (autumn berries)

Hardiness Fully hardy

Pyracantha

Firethorn is an important genus of tough, hardy, spiny, evergreen plants that need some protection from cold wind. Impressive yellow, orange or red berries that last all autumn and winter follow the cream-coloured flowers cascading from the branches in summer. A highly effective use for pyracanthas is as a hedge. *P. coccinea* 'Red Column' is an upright shrub with reddish shoots and vivid red autumn berries, and shows excellent resistance to fireblight. *P.* 'Knap Hill Lemon' is an unusual variety, worth growing for its clear yellow berries. *P.* 'Soleil d'Or' is a popular hybrid with hawthorn-like white flowers in late spring succeeded by golden-yellow berries in the autumn.

Height To 3m (10ft)

Flowering time Early summer (autumn berries)

Hardiness Fully hardy to frost hardy

Skimmia

This small genus includes several attractive shrubs, which bear scented flowers in spring and (on female plants) red berries in autumn, a fine contrast to the handsome, evergreen leaves. They are excellent in shrub or mixed borders or containers. They need moist, well-drained, humus-rich soil; most prefer shade. Young specimens of the male *S. japonica* 'Rubella' can be used in winter window boxes. *S.* x *confusa* 'Kew Green', a male selection with fragrant, cream flowers in early spring, tolerates full sun. *S. japonica* is the most widely grown species. It has distinctive narrow, glossy foliage and panicles of cream buds throughout winter that open to fragrant creamy-white flowers in spring. 'Rubella' is a male form with clusters of red buds through winter that open to dingy white flowers in early spring. 'Tansley Gem' is a female form, with a good crop of red berries.

Height To 6m (20ft)

Flowering time Spring (late summer and autumn berries)

Hardiness Fully hardy

above left to right
Photinia davidiana, berries of *Pyracantha coccinea* 'Red Column', and *Skimmia japonica* 'Redruth'.

below *Pyracantha* (firethorn) with autumn berrries.

climbers

above Fluffy clematis seedheads provide an attractive autumnal display.

Many autumn climbers provide flashy leaf colours before the foliage falls, as well as late season flowers, and extraordinary seedheads. And, of course, there are some excellent evergreens, which provide a beautiful contrast to fiery, deciduous foliage, and are especially welcome once that has fallen. Climbers can be grown up a wide variety of supports, including pillars and posts, trellises, walls (to which supporting wires have been attached if necessary), and trees.

Clematis

There are clematis varieties that flower in spring, summer and autumn. As well as those with autumn flowers, all have beautiful, long-lasting seedheads, like silvery tassels of silk. They look best when they catch the sun, often in early morning when they are covered by a few drops of dew. They have varied cultivation requirements, but all like moist, fertile, well-drained soil and most clematis prefer full sun. 'Bill Mackenzie' has bright yellow, thick-textured, lantern-like autumn flowers, which are followed by fluffy seedheads.
Height To 7m (23ft)
Flowering time All seasons, depending on variety
Hardiness Mostly fully hardy

below left to right
Clematis 'Bill Mackenzie' flowers and seedheads with an underplanting of fuchsia, *Hedera helix* 'Parsley Crested', and *Clematis tangutica,* flowers and seedheads.

C. tangutica

This species produces bright yellow, lantern-like flowers with pointed sepals and a prominent central boss of stamens, which are borne from midsummer to autumn and are followed by silky, silvery grey seedheads. There is much confusion between this species and the roughly similar *C. tibetana*, which will hybridize with it freely.
Height To 6m (20ft)
Flowering time Midsummer to autumn
Hardiness Fully hardy

Hedera

These self-clinging, evergreen climbers are among the most useful of garden plants. Though the species *H. helix* can be too rampant, it has many desirable cultivars which are more manageable. With their glossy leaves, all ivies provide excellent evergreen cover for trellis, walls and fences, and can also do well as ground cover in the dry soil under trees where little else will grow. Another attractive use is trailing over banks or climbing up poles and gates. From a design point of view, evergreen climbers form part of the garden structure, around which the rest of the garden changes. Ivies tolerate a range of conditions. Green varieties are happy in shade, but variegated types need more light and protection from cold winds.

H. helix

'Dragon Claw' is an attractive ivy with large, broad, five-lobed leaves, curling downwards, with closely fluted edges that turn red in winter. It is good for growing up walls and for ground cover. 'Parsley Crested' has rounded leaves that are crested at the edges and turn a beautiful bronze in cold weather. The long, strong-growing trailing stems make this a good ivy for flower arranging and hanging baskets. It looks good in a conservatory growing up a pillar or growing over an archway. 'Perkeo' has unusual puckered leaves that are light green and turn light red in cold weather; it is borderline hardy. 'Spetchley' is the smallest ivy available. Its small, three-lobed variable leaves, sometimes triangular, grow very densely. One of its main attractions is that the foliage changes with the first frost to a lovely wine colour. 'Spetchley' is a really hardy ivy. It grows best outdoors, either in a container or in the open garden.

Height To 10m (33ft)
Hardiness Mostly fully hardy

Parthenocissus

These foliage plants are grown mainly for their spectacular autumn colour. All the species described here cling by means of suckering pads and are excellent on walls. They need fertile, well-drained soil in shade or sun. *P. henryana* is sometimes called Chinese Virginia creeper. It has dark green leaves that are distinctively marked with central silvery white veins; they turn red in autumn. It grows to 10m (30ft) and is borderline hardy. *P. quinquefolia*, Virginia creeper, has vivid flame-red autumn leaf colour. It is eye-catching as cover for a large wall, and can also be dramatic weaving through the branches of a large tree, such as a silver birch.

Height To 15m (50ft)
Flowering time Summer (autumn foliage)
Hardiness Borderline to fully hardy

Vitis vinifera

Tenturier grape is the parent of the many varieties grown for edible crops and also of a number of purely ornamental selections. *V. v.* 'Purpurea' is one of the most widely grown. The leaves mature to purple, then develop even richer hues in the autumn as the blackish, unpalatable fruits ripen. This is excellent for growing up an average size wall. For larger walls, the rampant, vigorous *V. coignetiae* will reach a height of 15m (50ft). Vines like well-drained, neutral to alkaline, humus-rich soil in sun or partial shade.

Height 7.5m (25ft)
Flowering time Summer (autumn foliage)
Hardiness Fully hardy

above *Parthenocissus henryana* beginning to turn red at the start of autumn.

below left to right *Hedera helix* 'Spetchley', the red foliage of *Parthenocissus* and *Vitis vinifera* 'Purpurea'.

above *Acer griseum.*

below *Acer palmatum dissectum* 'Red Pygmy'.

trees

Autumn is an exciting season for trees: many deciduous ones offer sensational effects from richly coloured leaves, to brightly coloured berries, and those with attractive bark become more noticeable once they lose their leaves. Most medium-size gardens should have room for at least one kind.

Acer

Maples belong to a huge and important genus. There is one for every garden, large or small. *A. pseudo-platanus* (sycamore) is almost a weed in some gardens, but that should not blind you to the beauties of the other species. Maples suit a woodland planting or lightly shaded area, with fertile, well-drained soil.

A. griseum

A native of China, this slow-growing species is one of the most outstanding members of a fine genus. The leaves turn a brilliant red before they fall in autumn, but the principal interest is the cinnamon-red bark, which peels to reveal a richer colour beneath.
Height 10m (33ft)
Flowering time Spring (autumn foliage)
Hardiness Fully hardy

A. palmatum

Commonly known as Japanese maple, the species, which is native to Korea and China as well as to Japan, is a rounded tree or shrub displaying glorious autumn colour. *A. palmatum* f. *atropurpureum* (syn. 'Atropurpureum') is notable for the vibrant purple of its leaves, in spring and autumn. *A. palmatum* var. *dissectum* makes a dome-shaped tree with elegant ferny foliage, which turns red or yellow in autumn. It has a number of cultivars with coloured or variegated leaves. Acers in the Dissectum Atropurpureum Group have similar colouring to *A. palmatum* f. *atropurpureum* but with very finely dissected leaves, giving the plant a more filigree appearance. Slow-growing, they eventually make attractive, dome-shaped, spreading trees. 'Dissectum Nigrum' (syn. 'Ever Red') has finely dissected, blackish-purple leaves and forms a low, rounded bush. 'Fireglow' (syn. 'Effegi') carries rich burgundy-red leaves, which turn orange-red in the autumn. This requires some sun to enhance the leaf colour. 'Kagiri-Nishiki' (syn. 'Roseomarginatum') has pale green leaves margined with pink, later turning cream. 'Katsura' has the typical palm-shaped leaves of the species. Pale orange-yellow when young, they mature to a rich bronze, then redden in autumn. 'Ôsakazuki' carries mid-green leaves, which turn brilliant orange, crimson and scarlet in autumn. The red-tinted leaves of 'Rubrum' turn bright red in autumn. 'Sekimori' has very finely divided, filigree foliage, which is bright green, turning red or yellow in autumn.
Height 75cm–8m (2½–25ft)
Flowering time Spring (autumn foliage)
Hardiness Fully hardy

opposite from top, left to right *Acer palmatum* 'Fireglow', *A. palmatum* f. *atropurpureum* and *A. p.* 'Ôsakazuki', *A. p.* 'Sekimori', the bark of *A. griseum* and *A. palmatum* 'Karasugawa', *A. p.* 'Bloodgood', *A. p.* var. *dissectum* and *A. x conspicuum* 'Phoenix'.

Arbutus

A genus with many attractions, not the least of which are the charming, strawberry-like fruits that give the trees their common name of strawberry tree. (The fruits are edible, if insipid.) The lily-of-the-valley-like flowers, which appear at the same time as the ripening fruits, are also beautiful. Add peeling bark to the list of attractions, and the surprise is that they are not more widely planted. There are two main reasons for this: not all are reliably hardy, and some will grow well only in acid soil; they need shelter and full sun. *A. unedo* is an evergreen species that has a spreading, sometimes shrubby habit. It is native to south-eastern Europe and the Middle East. The white flowers appear in the autumn, at the same time as the strawberry-like fruits from the previous year ripen. The red-brown bark, which peels in shreds, is also an attractive feature. The form *A. u.* f. *rubra* reaches the same size as the species, but has deep pink flowers.
Height 6m (20ft)
Flowering time Autumn (autumn fruit)
Hardiness Mostly fully hardy

Cercidiphyllum

The genus contains a single species, which is native to western China and Japan. It is a choice tree for the garden grown for its spectacular autumn foliage. These trees do best in woodland conditions – in fertile soil in light dappled shade – and although they are tolerant of lime, the best autumn colour occurs on acid soil. *C. japonicum* var. *magnificum* (syn. *C. magnificum*), or the katsura tree, is a rare Japanese upright species with rounded leaves that turn yellow,

orange and red in autumn and winter and smell of toffee and burnt sugar when they fall to the ground. As the leaves start to fall they release a wonderful scent in a wide radius, up to 30m (100ft) away. It needs plenty of room, as it can reach 10m (33ft) high after 20 years; if it produces several stems, you can prune it to just one to limit its spread.
Height 10m (33ft)
Flowering time Spring (autumn foliage)
Hardiness Fully hardy

Cornus

Dogwoods are among the best trees for a small garden. Some are grown for their overall appearance and so make good specimens, while others have striking spring flowers and good autumn leaf colour. The genus also includes many shrubs and a few perennials. The different varieties suit a range of soils and locations.
Height To 10m (33ft)
Flowering time Late spring and early summer (autumn foliage)
Hardiness Fully hardy

Crataegus

Despite their ubiquity as roadside plants, hawthorns make excellent garden trees, particularly in exposed situations and on poor, limy soils. They are tough and hardy, in sun or partial shade, and make excellent hedges, particularly in country gardens.
Height To 12m (40ft)
Flowering time Late spring and early summer (autumn berries)
Hardiness Fully hardy

Ilex

Indispensable plants in any garden for their healthy, glossy leaves, the hollies are either trees or shrubs depending on age and how they have been pruned (if at all). If you inherit a garden with a large holly, think twice before ousting it – it will undoubtedly be of venerable age. Holly also makes an excellent hedge. Berries will be produced only on females, which will need a pollinating male nearby, so choose carefully among the cultivars. Those listed here are evergreen. *I. aquifolium*, native to northern Africa and western Asia as well as to Europe, often appears in gardens, but the many cultivars generally make more attractive plants. The following selections are all hardy. 'Aurea Marginata Pendula' is a slow-growing, rounded, weeping tree with purple stems and spiny, glossy, bright green leaves, margined with creamy yellow. It is a female form, producing red berries in autumn. It is an outstanding plant for year-round interest. The male 'Ferox Argentea' carries very prickly dark green leaves margined with cream. 'J. C. van Tol' is self-fertile, with bright red berries among the plain leaves.

'Silver Milkmaid', a female cultivar, has an open habit and leaves with white margins. The berries are scarlet. 'Silver Queen' (syn. 'Silver King'), which is a slow-growing male form, also has white-edged leaves. It has a dense, upright habit. All hollies can be shaped and topiarized; try vertical cylinders or pyramids. They can also be grown as windbreaks or provide shelter. Variegated forms prefer full sun.

Height To 25m (80ft)
Flowering time Spring to early summer (autumn berries)
Hardiness Fully hardy

Liquidambar styraciflua

A superb large tree for one of the best displays of autumn foliage colour. Plant it in an open area, where it can be seen from windows in the house. It likes moist, well-drained, acid to neutral soil; it produces the best leaf colour in full sun.

Height To 25m (80ft)
Flowering time Late spring (autumn foliage)
Hardiness Fully hardy

above *Liquidambar styraciflua* produces a brilliant display of russet autumn leaf colour.

below Bright red berries of *Ilex aquifolium* 'J. C. van Tol'.

above *Quercus* leaves.

gardens. They like moist, well-drained soil, preferably in full sun. In spring *M.* 'Evereste', a conical small hybrid, bears a profusion of large white flowers, opening from reddish-pink buds. The fruits, which develop in the autumn as the leaves turn yellow, are bright orange to red.
Height To 12m (40ft)
Flowering time Late spring (autumn fruits)
Hardiness Fully hardy

Malus

As well as all the apple trees (forms of *Malus domestica*), this genus includes the delightful crab apple. Though grown mainly for their ornamental value, crab apples can be cooked or made into jellies, and the trees make good pollinators for apple trees. They are compact and look good in cottage-style

Quercus

All the oaks are magnificent trees, and you shouldn't be put off by their final size. They stay small for quite a long time and can be pollarded to keep them within bounds, even if this prevents them from achieving their full splendour. Oak trees are important for wildlife, providing shelter for an enormous range of insects, birds and small mammals. Oaks should be grown in ordinary, well-drained soil, preferably in a sunny, open site. They tolerate light shade, but need space to expand. *Q. ilex*, a majestic evergreen, does particularly well in coastal situations. The variable leaves, often lance-shaped, are silver-grey when young, darkening to a glossy green as they age.

right *Malus* 'Evereste'.

far right *Malus* 'Golden Hornet'.

Q. robur, the common English oak, is a large species with the characteristically lobed leaves and clusters of acorns in autumn. More manageable in smaller gardens are some of the selections, including the shrubby 'Compacta', which is very slow growing. Also slow growing is 'Concordia' (golden oak), a small, rounded form carrying bright yellow-green leaves in spring. The neatly upright 'Hungaria' resembles *Populus nigra* 'Italica' (Lombardy poplar) in outline.

Height To 30m (100ft)
Flowering time Late spring and early summer (autumn foliage and acorns)
Hardiness Fully hardy

Sorbus

The rowans are splendid plants for cold gardens. They are hardy and provide valuable berries for birds in winter. Attractive flowers and outstanding autumn colour add to their appeal. Most prefer moist, well-drained neutral to acid soil, in sun or light shade, but *S. aria* tolerates dry, chalky soil.

S. aria

A large number of cultivars have been developed from this European species. 'Lutescens' has a more conical habit than the species and is thus better suited to small gardens. The leaves are covered in creamy-white hairs and are particularly brilliant as they emerge in spring. The heads of white flowers that appear in late spring are followed by dark red berries.

Height 10m (33ft)
Flowering time Late spring (autumn berries)
Hardiness Fully hardy

S. commixta

This compact tree, from Korea and Japan, is generally grown in the form 'Embley', which fruits rather more freely. The white spring flowers are followed by an abundance of brilliant orange-red berries at the same time as the leaves turn red.

Height 10m (33ft)
Flowering time Late spring (autumn berries)
Hardiness Fully hardy

S. mougeotii

This unusual small tree or shrub is native to mountainous regions of northern Europe. The broad leaves have greyish hairs on their undersides. The fruits, sometimes lightly speckled, turn red in autumn.

Height 4m (13ft)
Flowering time Late spring (autumn berries)
Hardiness Fully hardy

Stewartia monodelpha

A deciduous tree or shrub with peeling, grey and red-brown bark. The leaves give a superb autumn display when they turn red and orange before falling.

Height To 25m (80ft)
Flowering time Midsummer (autumn foliage)
Hardiness Fully hardy

above left to right
Sorbus hupehensis,
S. mougeotii and *Stewartia monodelpha.*

below *Sorbus* with autumn berries.

above left to right
Cryptomeria japonica
'Lobbii', *C. japonica,*
Taxodium distichum and
Taxus baccata 'Fastigiata'.

conifers

Once the summer flowers are over, conifers come into their own, both as a contrast to the colours of deciduous trees and shrubs, and later as welcome green features through the winter. There is a conifer for every size garden; they vary from neat, mounded dwarf forms, slow-growing, slim-line vertical trees which eventually reach 3m (10ft) high, to others with beautiful grey-blue foliage to monsters which grow 30m (100ft) high. They can be used to provide a wide range of effects including windbreaks on the garden boundary, ornamentals for their shape and coloured foliage, and architectural features adding extra interest from autumn to spring. They can be very effective in formal Italian or Eastern-style gardens.

Cryptomeria
Despite the common name, Japanese cedar, this monotypic genus (there is only one species) is found in China as well as Japan, albeit in two distinct forms. Japanese cedars will tolerate pruning and can even be coppiced or trained. They look good in Eastern or Japanese-style gardens, especially when they are grown to develop a gnarled trunk. Japanese cedars are among the most beautiful of all the conifers.

opposite top to bottom
Thuja orientalis 'Aurea
Nana', *Taxus baccata* 'Lutea',
Thuja occidentalis 'Ericoides'.

C. japonica
The species can reach a height of 25m (80ft) and is roughly columnar in shape. There are a huge number of cultivars available, suitable either as specimens or for use in rock gardens. All are hardy. 'Bandai-Sugi' is a slow-growing rounded dwarf form with blue-green foliage that bronzes well in cold winters. The intriguing 'Cristata' (syn. 'Sekka-sugi') has leaves that are curiously fused together, so that they resemble coral. 'Elegans' is potentially large and will form a broad obelisk; the trunk is often attractively curved. The wedge-shaped leaves are soft and bluish-green when young, turning a rich, glowing bronze in autumn. 'Lobbii' makes a handsome specimen in a large garden, forming a tall, slender, conical tree. The needle-like leaves are arranged in spirals. On mature specimens the thick, fibrous bark peels away. The cones age to brown. Rich, fertile soil is best, though they also grow on chalk. Prune in spring if necessary.
Height To 25m (80ft)
Hardiness Fully hardy

Taxodium
Swamp cypresses are among the most elegant of all conifers. Unfortunately, their eventual size rules them out for all but the largest gardens. They like moist or wet, preferably acid soil in full or partial shade. *T.*

distichum is a large, deciduous (though sometimes semi-evergreen) conifer that comes from the south-eastern United States. It forms a tall cone shape that becomes untidy as it matures. The needle-like leaves, which redden in the autumn producing an excellent display, are carried in two ranks. Mature plants produce the best colour. Purple male cones hang down and are a feature in winter; the female cones are inconspicuous. Near water it produces special breathing roots, which look like knees emerging from the ground around the trunk.
Height 40m (130ft)
Hardiness Fully hardy

Taxus

Yews are a valuable genus of conifers for the garden, with a range of foliage colour and habit. It grows in any well-drained, fertile soil, in sun or deep shade. Yew is widely used for hedging and topiary work, since, unlike most other conifers, it tolerates pruning and even seems to thrive on it. Even mature specimens will recover well if cut back hard. These conifers produce fleshy berries (usually red) rather than woody cones, which help to brighten up autumn and winter gardens. All parts are toxic; in some areas, there are restrictions on planting, particularly where cattle are being grazed.

T. baccata

A long-lived conifer, this is widely found in Europe and also in North Africa and Iran. Typically, it has blackish-green leaves, carried in a comb-like arrangement on the stems; male and female flowers are produced on separate plants, with berries, each containing a single seed, following on the females. Uncut, the yew forms a broad, spreading cone shape with dense horizontal branches, if unpruned. *T. b.* 'Lutea' has yellow berries. 'Fastigiata' (Irish yew), a female (and hence berry-producing) selection, is a familiar graveyard tree, forming an obelisk, pointed at the crown, but spreading with age. The stems are strongly upright. It can be kept within bounds by pruning and can also be wired into a narrower, more formal shape. It is an excellent choice for the small garden due to its limited size. It makes a good container plant. Yew also makes an excellent clean-cut hedge with nicely clipped sides, and various topiary shapes. They include everything from abstract geometric shapes to birds and beasts.
Height To 20m (70ft)
Hardiness Fully hardy

Thuja

These excellent conifers are similar to *Chamaecyparis* and are often mistaken for them, a distinction being that *Thuja* has aromatic foliage. They are just as good for hedging. Varieties include a number of coloured foliage forms. They like deep, moist, well-drained soil in full sun, and need shelter from very cold winds.

T. occidentalis

Although northern white cedar is not widely grown, it is the parent of a vast number of cultivars. 'Ericoides', a dwarf form, grows into a broad, sometimes rounded, obelisk. The spreading, scale-like leaves are green in summer, turning rich brown, sometimes purple, in autumn. As the name suggests, it combines well with heathers and is good in a rock garden.
Height To 20m (70ft)
Hardiness Fully hardy

T. orientalis 'Aurea Nana'

This is an appealing dwarf selection of a much larger species from China and Iran. It makes an egg-shaped plant, with yellowish-green, scale-like leaves held in irregular, vertical, fan-like plates; they tinge bronze in cold weather in autumn. The cones are flagon-like and bluish-green, maturing to grey. An excellent choice for a small garden, it associates well with heathers and other yellow-leaved shrubs. It can be grown in large pots or tubs, in old kitchen sinks, raised beds and rock gardens. It is so slow growing that even after many years it is unlikely to reach its full height.
Height 60cm (2ft)
Hardiness Fully hardy

AUTUMN DISPLAYS

You can create all kinds of effects in the autumn garden, from the quiet and gently atmospheric to the bold and bright. The scores of berries that start appearing now on shrubs and trees will, with luck, be with you until midwinter, keeping the garden interesting and colourful. Autumn is a marvellous time for reassessing the garden, and starting to make plans for the new year. It is the time to fill gaps where you need more late season interest and plant trees, shrubs and hedging, as well as bulbs that will flower the following spring.

left A beautiful glade of Japanese maples with a stunning display of foliage colour in bright reds, burnt oranges and golden yellow hues.

right One of the most exciting ways to use coloured foliage is near the edge of a pond or stream, where the colours of the leaves are reflected in the water.

far right Autumn fall at its best with dazzling red, orange and gold leaves of Japanese maples.

foliage colour

Autumn can be a spectacular time in the garden, with foliage in a range of colours, from purples and crimsons to gold and palest yellow. Some deciduous trees and shrubs merely turn a dull brown, however, so you need to choose the varieties carefully to get the best show. Even for a tiny garden, you are sure to find a shrub, climber or tree that will give a good display.

Why do leaves change colour?

The prime cause is dying leaf tissue, but the precise factors at work are not fully understood. The chlorophyll levels, which give leaves the dominant green colour, fall, revealing previously obscured pigments, including red, orange, yellow and purple.

right This maple, with its bright yellow leaves, is a centrepiece of the autumn garden.

The red pigment is at its strongest now, in the autumn. All this is triggered by shorter days, reduced light levels, falling temperatures, and high winds. The degree of brilliance varies from plant to plant, and is influenced by autumn light levels, night temperatures, soil fertility, and the length of the preceding winter. So if the colours in your garden change from year to year, that is the reason why.

Even if the display varies annually, depending on the conditions, some trees and shrubs are a must for the autumn garden. One reliable performer is the katsura tree (*Cercidiphyllum japonicum* var. *magnificum*), whose leaves turn brilliant orange and then give off the scent of toffee as they fall to the ground.

The many forms of Japanese maple (*Acer palmatum*) are also perennially popular, and produce a variety of gorgeous rich colours. Some are small enough to grow in containers, and so are ideal for small gardens.

above Fiery shades of reds and yellows, set off by the low sun, lend autumn a vibrant glow.

left The woods are at their most beautiful in the mellow midday autumn sun – a good time to collect the fruits of the season.

autumn berries

A big display of autumn berries provides a striking seasonal note and also adds a range of colours, from bright red to yellow and white. In time most, except the toxic ones, will get eaten by birds. Meantime, as the autumn mists descend and then lift, they will reveal beautiful clumps of tiny coloured balls high up in the trees and down on the ground, attracting extra wildlife.

trees and shrubs

The best berrying trees include ash (*Sorbus*), which provide a range of coloured fruit and several specimens that will not grow too high. The slow-growing *Sorbus x kewensis* only grows 2.5m (8ft) high and 2m (6ft) wide, and its late spring flowers are replaced by bright red berries. *Sorbus cashmiriana* eventually grows much higher, reaching 8m (25ft), but it will take over 20 years to do so. It has white berries with a black dot or eye. If you have room for a slightly taller tree, try *S.* 'Joseph Rock', which has yellow berries that become rich in colour towards the end of autumn.

left Ensure that attractive rosehips are prominently displayed, so that they can be fully appreciated.

above *Sorbus cashmiriana* has a mass of tiny white berries, which hang down in thick clusters.

Among berrying shrubs, pyracantha is one of the most prolific, with berries in many bright colours. Barberries produce blue-black fruits, *Gaultheria* has strikingly coloured magenta fruits and popular cotoneasters bear berries in many different colours.

rosehips

Many roses have outstanding hips, these include *Rosa moyesii* and *R. rugosa,* which make excellent hedges and have large, rich red flowers. They are disease-free, tough and hardy, and grow extremely well in sandy soils by the sea. The purple-rose flowers of *R. moyesii* start opening in early summer. The light pink flowers of *R. macrophylla* are eventually replaced by incredibly striking, long hips. The climbing *R. helenae* grows 6m (20ft) high; train some stems to dangle out of a large tree so that they clearly display their orange-red fruit.

above Pyracanthas provide a mass of small flowers in the summer, and these are followed by richly coloured autumn berries.

left Roses are excellent all-round shrubs or climbers, adding colour, scent (with the right choice), and attractive autumn rosehips from varieties such as 'Hansa', which are full and red.

seedheads and bark

Many plants have wonderful seedheads, which can be just as attractive as flowers. *Clematis tangutica* and *C. 'Bill Mackenzie'* both produce large fluffy balls of silvery silk that look exquisite when lit by the sun, especially when growing up through a tree.

One of the few plants with brightly coloured seedheads is *Physalis alkekengi*, the Chinese lantern. This perennial has vivid red or orange "paper lanterns", which can be cut and used in dried arrangements. For a wildflower garden, teasel (*Dipsacus fullonum*) is a must: its shapely, architectural seedheads not only look imposing but provide valuable food for birds. Poppies and thistles also add interesting shapes to the garden.

above and below right Clematis provide some of the most exciting seedheads in the garden. Those of 'Bill Mackenzie' and *C. tangutica* are at their best when covered with dew or lit by the sun.

above right Grasses, such as *Stipa tenuissima* in a naturalistic planting, look good planted with late perennials and architectural seedheads.

end of summer and in autumn, exposing the most exquisite bark beneath which is patterned cream, russet and grey. In fact the eucalyptuses offer some of the fastest growing trees, many with excellent bark. Quite a few species of tree can be kept shorter than they would otherwise grow by coppicing or pollarding. Those with attractive bark include *E. coccifera* (grey with white), *E. deanei* (pale yellow, grey and hints of red), the crooked, multi-stemmed *E. pauciflora* subsp. *debeuzevillei* (mottled like *E. p.* subsp. *niphophila*, but peeling in patches, not strips), *E. fraxinoides* and *E. gresoniana* (both white), and *E. viminalis* (white and reddish-pink).

Stewartias are much slower growing, and the best include *S. pseudocamellia* and *S. sinensis*. Both have colourful bark which turns dark reddish-brown before it begins to flake, exposing the new bark beneath. The foliage on both also turns bright red before falling.

bark

If you visit any arboretum in winter you will quickly see how many trees have amazing bark. The range includes bark which keeps peeling back in papery scrolls, revealing fresh new bark beneath, such as *Acer griseum*, and trunks which have quite beautiful colours.

The most popular trunks are gleaming bright white, for example *Betula utilis* var. *jacquemontii*, and they are dramatic on sunny autumn and winter days. 'Grayswood Ghost' has glossy leaves, the fast-growing 'Jermyns' has rounded leaves and large catkins (pussy willows), and 'Silver Shadow' has large, drooping dark green leaves: all three have particularly brilliant bark. As the white bark gets dirty, which invariably happens, you can even clean it with buckets of hot water to bring out the striking colour.

Another tree that is well worth growing for its bark is *Prunus serrula* with its smooth, shiny, and dark brown mahogany trunk. It eventually grows to 10m (33ft) high. If you have room, grow *Eucalyptus pauciflora* subsp. *niphophila* which has shedding white bark at the

above left *Acer griseum* is a constant attraction with its peeling strips of bark.

above The wonderfully patterned bark of *Stewartia* is displayed as the surface peels away to reveal new colours underneath.

left As this cherry tree expands from the middle, the old bark starts to peel off in papery strips.

above A country garden with *Vitis coignetiae* over a pergola, *Parthenocissus* and chrysanthemums.

top right A gravel garden, with shapely grasses, looks good even at the end of the year.

above right Conifers come in a wide choice of colours and shapes.

opposite *Aster novae-angliae* 'Alma Potschke' and fennel glowing in the mellow autumn sun.

autumn ideas

It is a good idea to go round the garden in autumn and see which areas could be livened up with new plants. Start by simply ensuring that you have plenty of late-flowering plants, such as asters, chrysanthemums, dahlias and autumn-flowering clematis. Fuchsias also have a wonderfully long season.

Colourful foliage is another essential feature, especially on climbers, and a novel way of letting everyone see it is by training the likes of *Vitis* and *Parthenocissus* over a pergola. In fact the sensational colours are even more exciting when you are standing underneath, on a sunny day, looking up at the sky through a thick film of orange and red. However, gardens do not have to rely just on bright colours for interest. Areas covered in gravel with specimen evergreens and grasses chosen for their architectural interest add interest. They will be just as attractive in autumn as in spring and summer, perhaps more so if the grasses have beautiful beige flowerheads.

Conifers are also extremely useful, coming in all shapes and sizes from dwarf varieties to the pencil thin 'exclamation marks', which can be used to create formal Italian-style gardens. They can be used as dividers and focal points, and have a surprising range of different coloured foliage: all shades of deep or bright green, soft pale blue-grey, brilliant yellow and even coppery bronze.

Besides adding new plants, the autumn is a good time of year to see exactly where artificial constructs would add interest to the garden, including statues, pillars, pergolas and gazebos.

borders

All beds and borders need star performers for each season, providing a continuation of shape and colour. There are scores of first-rate autumn plants, including dahlias, cannas and Japanese anemones, while many grasses are now at their best. *Cortaderia* (pampas grass) has lavish plumes of spikelets in late summer and autumn, and is a magnificent eye-catching compensation for the absence of summer flowers.

Other grasses, such as *Molinia*, are not as immediately dramatic but their green strappy leaves will soon turn an astonishing orange-brown, and when they are placed to catch the setting sun look like they are about to ignite. Deftly placed contrasting yellow rudbeckias add an extra richness.

left Autumn-flowering heathers can be used to create a vibrant, many-coloured tapestry in the garden.

above When allowed to multiply naturally, cyclamen will in time produce a carpet of pink and white flowers.

left *Cortaderia selloana* 'Sunningdale Silver' looks stunning when planted against contrasting dark plants.

below *Molinia caerulea* ssp. *caerulea* 'Variegata' and *Rudbeckia* make an appealing duo in this perennial border.

bulbs

Autumn bulbs provide as much fun and colour as the spring ones, and can be spectacular when naturalized under trees or on a bank. One of the very best is the hardy *Cyclamen coum*, which flowers in shades of purple-magenta, pink and white. The most eye-catching forms include the red flowering 'Nymans' and the white 'Album'.

patchwork colours

Heathers provide a big boost to the autumn garden because they are still flowering when many border plants are dying down. Even better, they have different coloured foliage, and because most grow to a fairly uniform height up to 60cm (24in), they can be used to provide a flowing tapestry. Create a special bed with two or three focal points.

right Cloud pruning is a Japanese technique, stripping branches of foliage, leaving clumps at the end.

topiary

The moment the summer garden starts to fade, the key architectural ingredients start to grab the eye. And some of the best are topiarized shapes that range from traditional birds, urns and simple geometric shapes, to clouds, animals, chairs, and even cars.

do-it-yourself topiary

below Two strong, sturdy cones add immediate shape and style to this garden and will create extra interest during the autumn and winter months.

The best way to decide where to place your topiary is to walk round the garden on a late autumn afternoon when it is looking quite bare, and decide where it really needs livening up. Topiary invariably works best as surprise features. It is remarkably simple to grow your own. Start with a sturdy 30cm (12in) high *Buxus*

(box) cutting. You can prune it in the spring to the desired shape, or to make a spiral, wait until the plant reaches the height you want, then start making cuts. You can either cut it by eye, or use a piece of string and run it round the plant so that you have a line to follow. Thereafter trim once in the spring and autumn to keep it looking smart and stylish.

To make a more elaborate, intricate shape, grow the box cutting inside a strong 3-D frame. Get one made to your design by a blacksmith, or buy one ready made. Stand it over the plant, and clip the growth as it pokes through. Again, trim it twice a year.

You can also create a topiarized hedge, turning one into a battlemented wall with windows, doors and turrets. Some types of conifers, such as yew, respond well to being cut back and provide a dense,

even surface. If you want really quick results, however, you might consider using *Leylandii*, which grows at 1m (3½ft) per annum in its early years. It will make an effective topiarized shape, smooth and solid, but you will have to be prepared to clip it very frequently to keep it looking neat. *Cryptomeria japonica* is suitable for "cloud" pruning, a Japanese technique which can be applied to a range of shrubby plants. Prune the plant to leave a limited number of stems, strip off their lower leaves and create geometric shapes at the ends. You can even apply this to a *Leylandii*, reducing it to three or four vertical stems, each one having a ball of bright green at the top, swaying in the wind.

above Box can be clipped to create beautiful, stylish shapes.

left An inventive chair-shaped piece of topiary, with a flat base to sit on.

shapes, and classical Italian-style containers with decorative touches. One large container is important as a focal point, and elaborate ceramic or stone urns always have plenty of impact.

Modest terracotta pots can be given a new lease of life by painting them in different colours. Think carefully about which colours to use, since coloured paint can stand out quite differently from the colours of plants. Pots can be decorated to your own taste, perhaps with narrow or broad stripes, for example in blue and white, pale green and yellow, or with vivid speckling on a bright background. These colours will not be evident in the summer when the flowers and leaves bush out and hang down, but they will show from mid-autumn when they inject extra life to patios and terraces.

above Simple terracotta pots are the perfect foil for the bright pink cyclamen flowers.

right The muted blue-grey and purple of ornamental cabbage is given added interest by a shiny, galvanized steel container.

opposite A group of containers is used here to stunning effect with *Erica gracilis*, *Skimmia japonica* 'Rubella' and *Gaultheria procumbens*.

containers

The imaginative use of containers is an excellent way of prolonging the growing season. Many plants are suitable for an autumn display, including a wide range of evergreens, small deciduous shrubs (for foliage and berries), late-flowering perennials such as asters or sedum, bulbs and ornamental cabbages. Good choices of bulbs are cyclamen in small containers and cannas in large ones. Heathers and skimmia make good container shrubs and even certain maples can be planted in large pots.

Check that the pots are clean and attractive in their own right because now, in the autumn, as the plants start to die back and they are less lush and abundant, they can become a prominent feature. Stone troughs always look good even when the plants have died down. Galvanized steel containers and buckets add a bright, modern look, and look good with plants whose leaves turn reddish-purple, or evergreens with shapely, shiny leaves. If you can afford it, it is also worth investing in a few really attractive pots, such as Victorian-style pots, with their different

AUTUMN TASKS

This is an extremely busy time of year with plenty of important tasks. The garden needs to be tidied up before winter, with all the debris swept away. Beds and borders need a final weeding, tender plants need digging up to be put in pots over winter, perennials need cutting back from now to the end of the season, ponds need clearing out, and the vegetable garden can be dug over. It is also a time for planting trees, shrubs and bulbs. Note this year's successes and failures, and what you intend doing differently when next summer takes off again.

left Dead leaves, particularly large ones like *Gunnera,* which are less likely to blow away, can be used to cover any perennials that need protection from frost.

early autumn

The weather in early autumn is still warm enough to make outdoor gardening a comfortable experience. Although the vibrant flowers of summer may be gone, there are plenty of delights to be enjoyed in the form of late-flowering gems such as nerines and chrysanthemums, not to mention the bright berries.

Apart from planting bulbs, and protecting frost-tender plants, there are few really pressing jobs at this time of year. You should, however, move any evergreen shrubs that need repositioning. Also dig up and divide any overgrown and congested perennials. Make sure that you have enough clean pots when it comes to potting up the tender plants which cannot be left outside in the frost and the wet. Pay close attention to the lawn. Go over it with a fork, stabbing it with the prongs to aerate it.

Early autumn is also the ideal time to start planning next spring's display of bulbs in beds, borders and containers.

above Bubble insulation on the inside of the glass panes will save money if you heat your greenhouse during the colder months.

the flower garden

❖ Plant spring-flowering bulbs
❖ Take fuchsia and pelargonium cuttings
❖ Sow hardy annuals to overwinter (only in mild areas or if you can provide winter protection)
❖ Plant lilies
❖ Plant up a spring window box, container or pot with bulbs
❖ Clear summer bedding and prepare for spring bedding plants
❖ Continue to watch for pests and diseases on roses and other vulnerable plants
❖ Disbud dahlias and chrysanthemums as necessary
❖ Lift and store dahlias after the first frost
❖ Lift and store gladioli and other tender bulbs, corms and tubers
❖ Take in tender aquatic plants from the pond if frost is threatened

plants at their best

❖ *Anemone* x *hybrida*
❖ *Aster novae-angliae*
❖ *Aster novi-belgii*
❖ *Chrysanthemum*
❖ *Dahlia*
❖ *Hibiscus syriacus*
❖ *Nerine bowdenii*
❖ *Pyracantha*
❖ *Rudbeckia*
❖ *Salvia uliginara*
❖ *Sedum spectabile*
❖ *Sorbus*
❖ *Sternbergia lutea*

above You can pack more bulbs into a window box by planting in layers. Place large bulbs such as daffodils or tulips at the lower level and add potting soil.

above Position smaller bulbs such as scillas and crocuses on top of the larger bulbs. Try to position them so that they lie between the larger bulbs.

above Plant a container of evergreens for autumn and winter, and add some early-flowering bulbs to brighten up the display in late winter and early spring.

the greenhouse and conservatory

❖ Bring in house and greenhouse plants that have been standing outdoors for the summer

❖ Sow spring-flowering plants such as cyclamen, schizanthus and exacums

❖ Clean off summer shading washes

❖ Repot cacti if necessary

❖ Check that the greenhouse heaters are in good working order. Arrange to have them serviced, if necessary

❖ Pot up and pot on seedling pot-plants as it becomes necessary

❖ Plant hyacinths for early flowering under glass

above To plant lilies, dig an area of soil to a depth of 20cm (8in), large enough to hold four or five bulbs. Add coarse grit or sand.

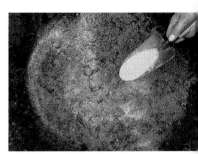

above Add a sprinkling of bonemeal or a controlled-release fertilizer.

above To preserve and store garden canes, knock off most of the soil, then scrub with a stiff brush and garden or household disinfectant.

above Collect old bedding plants to transfer to a compost heap. Being non-woody they rot down easily. Make sure that there are no seeding or perennial weeds.

above Space the bulbs about 15cm (6in) apart and make sure that they are deep enough to be covered with about twice their own depth of soil.

above To revive a lawn in poor condition, apply an autumn lawn feed.

above Pack dahlia tubers in a well-insulated box with vermiculite, wood shavings, peat substitute, sand or crumpled newspaper placed between them. Keep in a frost-free location.

mid-autumn

This is an unpredictable time of year. In cold regions quite severe frosts can suddenly strike, while in mild climates some plants are still growing and tender plants may go on flowering for a while. This is the time to listen to the weather forecast and to be on the alert, in particular, for frost warnings. Mid-autumn is the time to create and dig over any new flower beds for next spring, weeding them carefully. Collect seed from flowers, keeping it dry until sowing. Dahlias should be lifted now. Once the leaves are blackened by frost, dig them up, cut off the stems, turn them upside down in a frost-free place to dry, and then store over winter in a box of vermiculite or other suitable material. They will need an occasional sprinkling of water so that they do not dry out.

the flower garden

❖ Make a new lawn from turf or seed
❖ Give an established lawn autumn care treatment
❖ Plant bare-root and potted trees, hedges, roses and shrubs
❖ Plant herbaceous plants
❖ Divide over-large herbaceous plants
❖ Clear summer bedding
❖ Plant spring bulbs
❖ Protect vulnerable plants and shrubs when frost is threatened
❖ Cut down and lift dahlias blackened by frost
❖ Lift gladioli corms
❖ Sow sweet peas in pots
❖ Take tender fuchsias, pelargoniums and chrysanthemums indoors for the winter
❖ Prepare the pond for winter
❖ Take in tender aquatics

above Net or rake out submerged oxygenating plants such as elodea so that they do not clog the pond.

above Remove tender aquatic plants such as *Salvinia auriculata*. Keep them in a plastic container with water.

above Protect a pond from falling autumn leaves by stretching a fine-mesh net over it. Remove leaves regularly.

the greenhouse and conservatory

❖ Clean and disinfect, ready for winter
❖ Insulate
❖ Remove yellowing and dead leaves from plants to prevent pests and diseases overwintering
❖ Check that heaters are working properly
❖ If you do not have a maximum-minimum thermometer, buy one
❖ Ventilate whenever the weather is mild enough
❖ Clean out all pots before storing away

above As a space saving alternative to keeping large plants indoors over winter, pelargoniums can be cut down and stored in trays of damp potting mix. The trays should be at least 15cm (6in) deep.

above Apply moss killer if the lawn needs it. Use one recommended for autumn use only.

above If you have a lot of leaves, putting them in a wire netting container is an excellent way to make leaf mould: simply leave them uncovered, to rot down.

above If a shrub rose was unpruned when bought, cut back all the shoots to 15–20cm (6–8in) above the ground.

above Autumn is the best time to plant a new hedge. Check planting distances and depths and water well.

plants at their best

❖ *Acer*
❖ *Amelanchier kamarckii*
❖ *Anemone* x *hybrida*
❖ *Aster novi-belgii*
❖ *Berberis*
❖ *Cotinus* 'Grace'
❖ *Cotoneaster*
❖ *Fothergilla*
❖ *Gaultheria*
❖ *Liriope muscari*
❖ *Parthenocissus*
❖ *Pyracantha*
❖ *Schizostylis coccinea*

late autumn

A last-minute spurt of action is often needed at this time of year, to get the garden ready for winter and ensure protection for plants that need it. In many areas the cold will already have taken its grip, but in warmer climates there are still mild days to be enjoyed.

Besides tackling the many jobs described here, the autumn is also a good time of year to think of redesigning the garden. While most plants are dormant you can put up pergolas and arches, build walls, design new beds, lay paths (avoiding areas where they will get covered by leaves which become mushy and slippery in wet weather) and dig ponds. It is better that new ponds are left to be filled by rainwater over winter, thus avoiding the chemicals in tap water, which can lead to the growth of quick-spreading algae.

The autumn is also an excellent time to start ordering new seed catalogues. With everything still fresh in the mind, you'll know what needs to be grown where next year, what is not worth trying a second time, and which areas of the garden need to be spruced up.

above Pot up a few mint roots to prolong the season and for early leaves next spring. Keep them in the greenhouse.

the flower garden

❖ Cut down the dead tops of herbaceous perennials
❖ Clear garden refuse and leaves and put in the compost bin
❖ Remove pumps from the pond, clean and store in a dry place for the winter
❖ Plant bare-root and potted trees, hedges, shrubs and roses
❖ Clear summer bedding if not already done so
❖ Finish planting spring bulbs as soon as possible
❖ Plant tulip bulbs
❖ Protect vulnerable plants that remain in the garden
❖ Bring tender chrysanthemums indoors if not already done so
❖ Prune berry bushes
❖ Take hardwood and softwood shrub cuttings
❖ Prepare the pond for winter
❖ Remove leaves that have fallen on rock plants
❖ Cover alpines that need protection from winter wet with a pane of glass
❖ Protect the crowns of vulnerable herbaceous plants such as lupins from slugs

plants at their best

❖ *Acer*
❖ *Berberis*
❖ *Cotoneaster*
❖ *Fothergilla*
❖ *Gaultheria*
❖ *Iris foetidissima*
❖ *Liriope muscari*
❖ *Nerine bowdenii*
❖ *Pyracantha*
❖ *Schizostylis coccinea*

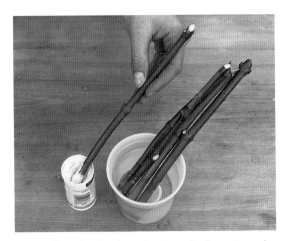

above After taking hardwood cuttings, dip the moistened base end of each cutting into a rooting powder.

above Plant hardwood cuttings over a layer of sharp sand, 8–10cm (3–4in) apart, leaving 3–5cm (1–2in) above ground.

above Lift clumps of chives and pot up for an extended season. Divide the clumps if necessary.

above Scrub old pots and containers inside and out with a disinfectant to ensure they are disease-free.

above Prune soft fruit bushes to about 23–30cm (9–12in) after planting. This stimulates new growth from the base.

the greenhouse and conservatory

❖ Clean and disinfect, ready for the winter
❖ Insulate
❖ Ventilate whenever the weather is mild enough. This is vital to keep air circulating and eliminate diseases such as botrytis, which flourishes in damp, still air
❖ Except with winter-flowering plants that are still in strong, active growth, gradually give plants less water. Most will then tolerate low temperatures better and disease should be less of a problem
❖ It is not too late to sow cyclamen seed for flowering the following Christmas
❖ Throw out empty seed packets, and give the greenhouse a final check, cleaning any equipment being stored away, especially spades and trowels

above After lifting chrysanthemums, trim the roots and then store in a tray with about 3cm (1in) of soil.

above Disinfect the frame and staging of a greenhouse, to prevent pests and diseases overwintering.

the winter garden

CREATING A WINTER GARDEN

Winter gardens can be extraordinarily beautiful. They may lack colourful beds and borders, but they often have a subtler, more satisfying attraction. There is, of course, no lack of colour if you look closely. Many trees and shrubs bear vivid red, yellow or orange berries, and there are plenty of bulbs that flower in the depths of winter. Evergreen plants and conifers provide form and texture in every shade of green. It is in winter, however, that the underlying structure of the garden can be appreciated. Unclothed pergolas and trellises can be admired, while ornaments, such as terracotta urns and stone sundials, can be enjoyed for themselves.

left Hellebores, which are available in a wide range of colours, produce a superb winter display. Grow them in large clumps for a striking effect.

right *Cornus alba* 'Sibirica' is one of the best dogwoods for bright winter colour. Give it a sunny, prominent position.

WINTER GARDENS CAN EASILY BE BRIGHTENED up. When you are planning your garden, think about the effect that you want to achieve in winter, not just about how the individual plant will look when it is in full bloom or leaf. Most herbaceous perennials die back in autumn, but there is a vast range of other plants, from trees and shrubs, both deciduous and evergreen, to tiny bulbs, that can be used to provide interest all winter long.

choosing colour

The winter garden can be a mass of colour. Early-flowering bulbs, such as *Crocus sieberi* and its cultivars, can be allowed to naturalize in grass to provide a carpet of colour. In late winter, the tiny *Iris reticulata* has rich purple flowers, splashed with yellow.

below The easily grown, 12cm (5in) high *Iris* 'George' starts flowering at the end of winter.

I. danfordiae, another early flowerer, has scented yellow blooms. *I. foetidissima* has bright red winter seeds, and with luck the violet-blue *I. unguicularis* (syn. *I. stylosa*) might be in flower before Christmas day if there has been a long, hot summer.

Colourful berries abound on many forms of cotoneaster and holly. If they are not eaten by birds, the red berries of *Cotoneaster horizontalis* last until midwinter, and the yellow berries of *C. salicifolius* 'Rothschildianus' last well into winter. If you want holly berries, make sure you plant both male and female forms or a self-fertile form.

fragrant flowers

High summer may be the time of roses, lavender and honeysuckle, but among the delights of a well-planned winter garden will be the subtle aromas of carefully selected shrubs and bulbs, all the more welcome for being unexpected. Look out especially for viburnums and daphnes. The deciduous *Viburnum* x *bodnantense*, for example, bears strongly scented white to pink flowers from autumn to spring, while the evergreen *Daphne odora* has clusters of fragrant, purplish-pink to white flowers from midwinter to spring.

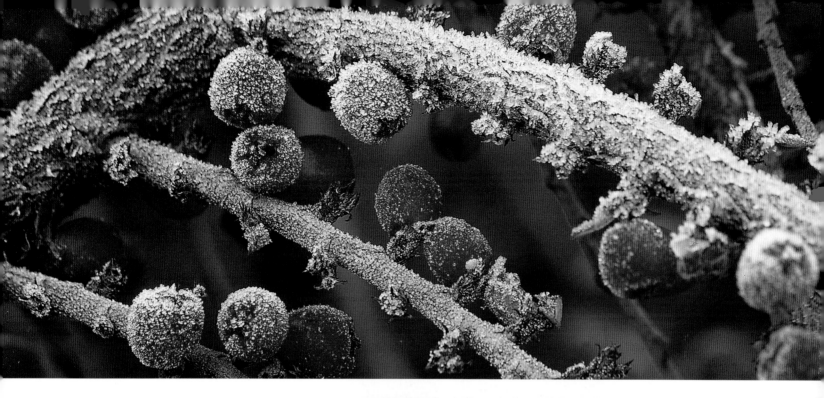

The reliable *Hamamelis* spp. (witch hazel) produce their unusual, spidery but scented flowers on the leafless branches from early winter into late spring, seemingly unaffected by the harshest of weather. Less well known is *Sarcococca humilis* (sweet box). Plant this evergreen shrub near a path or door so that you can enjoy the sweet scent of the pink-flushed, white flowers in midwinter.

beautiful bark

It is easy to overlook the attractive bark of many trees, which is often visible only in winter. Perhaps the most exciting of the trees with interesting bark is the compact *Prunus serrula*. It has smooth, rich red-brown bark, which peels to reveal gold-coloured bands.

Tilia platyphyllus 'Rubra' (red-twigged lime) also provides vibrant winter colour. The mass of bright red, twiggy growth at the top of the tree looks sensational when the ground below is covered with snow. Among the best of the white-barked trees is the lovely birch, *Betula utilis* var. *jacquemontii* 'Silver Shadow'. Look out, too, for shrubs with colourful shoots. One of the best is *Cornus alba* (red-barked dogwood), which has extraordinary, bright red new stems.

above Bright frost-covered red berries of *Cotoneaster frigidus* 'Cornubia'.

left There is room for the shiny, brown-stemmed *Prunus serrula* even in a medium-sized garden. Grow it as a feature plant where it can be easily seen.

WINTER PLANTS

The best way to see the full range of winter plants is to visit a well-stocked garden centre or nursery between the end of autumn and early spring. It is also worth visiting well-maintained, first-rate public gardens. Take a notebook with you so that you do not forget the plants that appeal to you. Some of the best known and most reliable bulbs, perennials and shrubs are described and illustrated on the following pages. There is also advice on where and how to grow them so that you get the best results every time.

left *Cornus stolonifera* 'Flaviramea' is a great choice for winter gardens because of its bright yellow, vertical stems. Grow plenty of clumps together for the most startling effect.

above *Crocus chrysanthus* 'Blue Pearl'.

below left to right
Chionodoxa forbesii 'Pink Giant', *Crocus tommasinianus* 'Ruby Giant' and *Crocus sieberi* 'Firefly'.

bulbs

There are many excellent bulbs for the winter garden. Always plant them in groups or, in a large garden, in drifts so they can naturalize.

Chionodoxa

Commonly known as glory of the snow, this is a genus of six species of bulbs found on mountainsides and forests in Crete, western Turkey and Cyprus. They are related to scillas. *Chionodoxa forbesii* 'Pink Giant' produces racemes of 4 to 12 star-shaped, pale pink flowers, 1–2cm (½–¾in) wide, with white centres.
Flowering height 15cm (6in)
Flowering time Late winter to mid-spring
Hardiness Fully hardy

Crocus

The crocus is one of the best-known late winter and early spring flowers. The genus embraces more than 80 species of dwarf corms found in a wide variety of locations, from central and southern Europe, northern Africa and the Middle East to central Asia and western China. Hundreds of cultivars have been produced. Almost every flower colour but pink is available, and some are attractively striped. A few have stamens in a contrasting colour. Robust hybrids are splendid for naturalizing in lawns, and they can create stunning effects, either in the traditional mixture of colours or when a more subtle selection of just one or two shades is planted.

C. chrysanthus

This species is usually represented in cultivation by its many selections, all flowering in late winter to early spring and including 'Advance', yellow with violet outer petals; 'Blue Pearl', which has silver-blue flowers; 'Ladykiller', which has slender, pure white flowers marked with purple; 'Snow Bunting', pure white; and one of the most spectacular cultivars, 'Zwanenburg Bronze', which has rich yellow flowers marked with purple-brown.
Flowering height To 7.5cm (3in)
Flowering time Late winter to early spring
Hardiness Fully hardy

C. sieberi

Flowering in late winter to early spring, this species has yellow-centred, light blue flowers with bright orange pistils. Among the prettiest forms are the golden-throated, white 'Albus' (syn. 'Bowles' White'),

which flowers in early spring, and 'Firefly', which has prolific lilac and yellow flowers.

Flowering height To 7.5cm (3in)
Flowering time Late winter to early spring
Hardiness Fully hardy

C. tommasinianus

This crocus is one of the best for naturalizing and produces lavender flowers in late winter. 'Ruby Giant' has large, purple flowers; 'Whitewell Purple' has purplish-red flowers, but with silvery-mauve lining inside and it is more slender than those of 'Ruby Giant'.

Flowering height To 10cm (4in)
Flowering time Late winter to early spring
Hardiness Fully hardy

C. vernus

The species has many selections, all of which are excellent for naturalizing and flower from late winter to early spring. These include 'Jeanne d'Arc', which has pure white flowers; 'Pickwick', which has greyish-white flowers, striped with violet; and 'Remembrance', which has violet flowers with a silvery sheen.

Flowering height To 10cm (4in)
Flowering time Late winter to early spring
Hardiness Fully hardy

Cyclamen

The unmistakable flowers of these plants make a delightful carpet under deciduous trees and shrubs.

C. coum

This species flowers from late winter to mid-spring, in a range of colours, from purple-violet to pink and white. The nodding flowers often have darker staining towards the mouth. The attractive rounded leaves usually have silver markings. This species associates particularly well with snowdrops.

Flowering height 5–7.5cm (2–3in)
Flowering time Late winter
Hardiness Fully hardy

C. persicum

The scented flowers range in colour from white to a glowing cerise-red and appear in winter and spring. Some combine two colours on the frilly petals. The flowers have darker staining towards the mouth, and the heart-shaped leaves are often patterned. Many cultivars have been bred but look for those with a sweet scent and attractively marked foliage.

Flowering height 10–20cm (4–8in)
Flowering time Early winter to early spring
Hardiness Frost tender

above left to right This group of mixed crocuses, which includes *Crocus tommasinianus, C. chrysanthus* and *C. vernus,* has formed a natural-looking carpet of colour; *Cyclamen persicum* and *C. coum.*

below *Crocus sieberi* 'Albus' (syn. 'Bowles' White').

Eranthis

Commonly known as winter aconite, this is one of the earliest bulbs to flower. They are robust enough to penetrate a light covering of snow, which is a charming effect when it occurs. Like snowdrops, they transplant best when putting on growth after flowering, so when buying them look for plants "in the green". They are good for carpeting areas beneath deciduous trees. The flowers open only when the sun is shining. They soon form large clumps and naturalize quickly in ideal conditions, especially in alkaline soils.

The golden petals of *Eranthis hyemalis* are surrounded by a collar of deeply dissected green leaves.
Flowering height 5–7.5cm (2–3in)
Flowering time Winter
Hardiness Fully hardy

Galanthus

Few plants have the charm of the snowdrop or are as welcome. Each flower has six petals, the outer three longer than the inner ones. Unusually among bulbs, snowdrops seem to prefer slightly damp soil. Snowdrops associate well with winter aconite, winter-flowering heathers and dwarf *Reticulata* irises.

G. elwesii

This species is less well known than *G. nivalis*. It is a larger plant, with bright green, strap-shaped leaves and flowers with large green spots on the inner petals.
Flowering height 25cm (10in)
Flowering time Winter
Hardiness Fully hardy

G. nivalis

The best-known of the snowdrops and one that naturalizes easily. The bell-shaped, pure white flowers hang downwards, the outer petals flaring outwards to

reveal the green markings on the inner ones. 'Flore Pleno', the double form, is no less charming.
Flowering height 10cm (4in)
Flowering time Winter
Hardiness Fully hardy

G. 'S. Arnott'

Long, virgin-white flowers fall like rounded drops of snow from a slender stem. The three outer petals open to reveal three shorter inner petals, each with green markings at the base and apex.
Flowering height 2–4cm (¾–1½in)
Flowering time Late winter
Hardiness Fully hardy

Iris

This genus has more than 300 species of winter-, spring- and summer-flowering bulbs, rhizomes and perennials.

I. danfordiae

A dwarf species with scented, yellow flowers, 5cm (2in) across, which have green markings. They look effective with winter-flowering heathers.
Flowering height 10cm (4in)
Flowering time Late winter to early spring
Hardiness Fully hardy

I. reticulata

This dainty species from the Caucasus is one of the first bulbous plants to flower in the gardening year, producing its rich violet-blue, yellow-splashed flowers in late winter. Unfortunately, it is not reliably perennial, so plant fresh stock annually. Selections include 'George', which has deep purple flowers with a yellow stripe down the centre of the fall petal.
Flowering height 15cm (6in)
Flowering time Late winter
Hardiness Fully hardy

I. unguicularis

Algerian iris (syn. *I. stylosa*) is one of the harbingers of spring. It is unique in the genus and should be planted in every winter garden. Among the grassy foliage, elegant lilac-mauve flowers with yellow markings unfurl from scrolled buds as early as midwinter, the main flowering being in late winter to early spring. It needs a hot spot in well-drained soil: at the foot of a warm wall is ideal. For reliable flowering, the upper surface of the rhizome should be exposed to the sun and plants should be left undisturbed once established.
Flowering height 23–30cm (9–12in)
Flowering time Late winter to early spring
Hardiness Fully hardy

above *Iris danfordiae.*

below left to right
Iris reticulata 'George', *I. r.* 'Pauline' has dark violet flowers with distinctive white markings on the falls, and *I. unguicularis.*

perennials

Most perennials are dormant in winter and start shooting out of the ground in spring, so the ones that do flower in winter are eye-catching. The following provide an exciting glimpse of what can be grown in the winter garden, when many plants are resting.

Helleborus

This is an important genus from the gardener's point of view, with many desirable plants, all with nodding flowers and handsome, more or less evergreen leaves. They are indispensable in the winter garden. All hellebores thrive in the shade of deciduous trees and shrubs and will even tolerate heavy shade next to a wall. They are easy to grow in any fertile, well-drained soil (although most prefer heavy and alkaline conditions) in sun or shade. All are poisonous.

H. argutifolius

Corsican hellebore is a handsome species that tolerates drier conditions than most other members of the genus. The firm, jade-green leaves, which have toothed leaflets, are attractive throughout the year.

The clusters of apple-green, cup-shaped flowers appear in late winter and last until early spring. It is a splendid foil for *Iris reticulata* and early narcissi.
Flowering height 1m (3ft)
Flowering time Late winter and early spring
Hardiness Fully hardy

H. foetidus

Bear's foot or stinking hellebore is a dramatic species, which makes a clump of dark-green leaves. Strong stems carrying many bell-shaped, apple-green flowers (usually edged with maroon) appear in midwinter to mid-spring. It looks good with snowdrops. Plants of the Wester Flisk Group have red-tinged stems and leaf and flower stalks and grey-tinged leaves.
Flowering height 75cm (30in)
Flowering time Midwinter to mid-spring
Hardiness Fully hardy

H. niger

The Christmas rose is one of the prettiest and most desirable of the hellebores, but unfortunately, it is also one of the trickiest to grow. It has dark green, basal, leathery leaves and large, glistening, cup-shaped white flowers in early winter. The flowers are sometimes

flushed with pink, with greenish-white centres, ageing to pinkish-white. It is slow to establish and needs fertile, sticky soil that does not dry out. 'Potter's Wheel' is a desirable selection with larger flowers, as is *H. niger* subsp. *macranthus* with its bluish or grey-green leaves.

Flowering height 30cm (12in)
Flowering time Early winter to early spring
Hardiness Fully hardy

H. orientalis

The Lenten rose, an Eastern Mediterranean species, is one of the easiest hellebores to grow and is also one of the most variable species. The flowers, which appear from late winter into spring, can be white, yellowish-cream, dusky-pink, clear glowing red or plum-purple, and they can also be spotted inside with a different colour to varying degrees. All are flushed green inside and out. The leaves are also handsome: firm and with serrated edges, and in shades of green, paler leaves being associated with paler flower colours. Blackened leaves should be removed. Plant in clusters of 3–5 plants to make a striking statement.

Flowering height 45cm (18in)
Flowering time Midwinter to mid-spring
Hardiness Fully hardy

Ophiopogon

The species, *Ophiopogon planiscapus* (lilyturf), is rarely grown: it is a grass-like plant with dull, deep-green leaves and small, bell-shaped, pale pinkish-purple summer flowers, and produces small, black berries in autumn. Of greater interest are the cultivars, especially 'Nigrescens' (syn. *O.* 'Arabiscus'; 'Black Dragon'; 'Ebony Knight'), with striking, black-purple leaves and small, purplish, bell-shaped flowers. The plant spreads slowly by stolons. For the most impact, grow it in gravel or in containers. It is especially effective in a Japanese-style planting.

Flowering height 20cm (8in)
Flowering time Summer (winter leaves)
Hardiness Fully hardy

Phormium

Originally from New Zealand, phormiums look exotic but are frost hardy. Being evergreen, they add interest throughout the year. *P. tenax* 'Rainbow Queen' has a wide range of colours with its sword-like leaves ranging from pink and lemon through orange and bronze. It requires sun and moist soil.

Height 2–2.5m (7–8ft)
Flowering time Summer (winter leaves)
Hardiness Frost hardy

above left to right
Ophiopogon planiscapus 'Nigrescens', *Helleborus niger* 'Potter's Wheel' and *Phormium tenax* 'Rainbow Queen'.

above *Carex buchananii.*

below left to right *Carex hachijoensis* 'Evergold', *Elymus magellanicus* and *Carex flagellifera.*

grasses

Grasses have four good seasons of interest: in spring, when the bright new shoots start emerging, in summer, when they are at their peak and flower, in autumn, when many turn yellow and reddish, and in winter, because they should be left standing, so that their shapes add interest until being cut down at the end of the season.

Carex

Sedge is a large and important genus, containing about 1000 species, which are distinguished by their triangular stems. They are ideal bog garden plants, but some are also worth trying in mixed borders for their attractive mounds of leaves. Most are best in reliably moist soil in sun or light shade. *C. buchananii* is an elegant, clump-forming evergreen with narrow copper-coloured leaves that turn towards orange in the winter. *C. comans* 'Frosted Curls' is an evergreen, compact hybrid, which makes dense clumps of narrow, pale green leaves that curl at the tips. *C. conica* is from Japan and South Korea and is usually seen in gardens in an attractive form, C. c. 'Snowline', which makes neat clumps of dark green leaves strikingly margined

with white. This does well in ordinary garden soil and is useful for providing long-term interest at the front of a border; it is also effective in gravel. *C. flagellifera* makes a clump of arching, bronze-brown leaves, which are an excellent foil to green-, silver- or yellow-leaved plants. It will grow in almost any soil. *C. oshimensis* 'Evergold' (syn. *C. morrowii* 'Evergold') is an outstanding evergreen sedge with arching leaves, centrally banded with cream. It is an excellent plant for lighting up a winter garden. It prefers well-drained soil but will grow in sun or semi-shade. *C. testacea* is an evergreen sedge from New Zealand. The arching, pale olive-green leaves are tinged bronze.
Flowering height 30–60cm (12–24in)
Flowering time Midsummer (winter leaves)
Hardiness Borderline to fully hardy

Elymus

Wild rye or lyme grass is excellent as an infill in mixed or herbaceous borders. Grow these grasses in ordinary garden soil in sun or light shade. *E. magellanicus* is a clump-forming species, native to Chile and Argentina, and has spiky, steel-blue leaves. It is a good container plant.
Flowering height 15cm (6in)
Flowering time Summer (winter leaves)
Hardiness Fully hardy

Festuca

The genus contains about 300 perennial grasses, which produce attractive tufts of foliage. They are ideal for placing at the front of borders or among rock plants. *F. glauca*, blue or grey fescue, is one of the most popular grasses. It is an evergreen species, which makes tufts of steely-blue leaves that are still evident in winter. The summer flowers are an added bonus. It can also be grown in containers. It prefers moderately fertile, dry, well-drained soil in full sun. The many selections include 'Blaufuchs' (syn. 'Blue Fox'), which has bright blue leaves. The blue-green leaves of 'Harz' are tipped purple.

Flowering height 30cm (12in)
Flowering time Summer (winter leaves)
Hardiness Fully hardy

Hakonechloa macra

This hardy Japanese grass is usually represented in gardens by the attractive cultivars 'Aureola', which has green-striped, yellow leaves, and 'Alboaurea' (syn. 'Variegata'), which has green, white and yellow leaves. The leaves of 'Aureola' are flushed with red in autumn. They are clump-forming plants, which make rounded cushions of tapering foliage. Small flowers are borne in spikelets in summer and early autumn, and these persist into winter. It prefers a moisture-retentive soil in shade or part shade. It is one of the most attractive and versatile ornamental grasses, and is suitable for growing in containers on patios, in courtyard gardens, rock gardens, or at the front of a mixed or herbaceous border.

Height 45cm (18in)
Flowering time Summer and autumn (winter leaves)
Hardiness Fully hardy

Imperata

The six species of grass in the genus are grown for the beauty of their leaves rather than for their flowers, which appear only in areas with long hot summers. They make a good foil to a range of flowering plants in mixed borders. Grow in any reasonable soil, preferably moisture-retentive, in sun or light shade. Remove the seed heads to prevent self-seeding (and reversion to plain green). Some winter protection – a dry mulch of straw, for instance – is advisable in very cold climates. *I. cylindrica* 'Rubra' (syn. 'Red Baron'), Japanese blood grass, is usually found in the form of this attractive cultivar, whose name refers to the red colouring that the leaves develop from the tip downwards.

Height 1m (3ft)
Flowering time Summer (winter leaves)
Hardiness Half-hardy

above left to right *Festuca glauca, Imperata cylindrica* 'Rubra' and *Hakonechloa macra* 'Alboaurea'.

below As the name suggests, the leaves of *Carex* 'Frosted Curls' gently curl at the tips .

shrubs

An indispensable element of the winter garden, shrubs provide form, structure, fragrance and colour. A well-planted garden will have a selection of these useful plants, each contributing to the overall scheme. Topiarized evergreens and deciduous shrubs with scented winter flowers should be positioned where their characteristics can be appreciated to the full.

Chimonanthus

Commonly known as wintersweet, this is a genus of six species of evergreen and deciduous shrubs, although only one is widely grown and reliably hardy. Plant wintersweet where it will be hidden among summer-flowering shrubs.

C. praecox

This deciduous shrub is grown for the intensely fragrant, bell-shaped yellow flowers, stained brownish-red inside, which are borne in midwinter on bare stems. In summer glossy, mid-green leaves, each to 20cm (8in) long, cover the stems. The cultivar 'Grandiflorus' has larger, deeper yellow flowers.
Flowering height 4m (12ft)
Flowering time Winter
Hardiness Fully hardy

Cornus

The dogwoods include some enormous trees, for which you will need a large garden, but there are some shrubs, which can be kept small by coppicing them every year. This forces them to put up a number of short stems, about 3m (10ft) high, the best of which are richly coloured. The spring coppicing can either involve cutting back every single stem, or just half so that it always has some growth. The two species to look for are *C. alba* and *C. sanguinea* and their cultivars.
Height 3m (10ft)
Flowering time Late spring and early summer (coloured winter stems)
Hardiness Fully hardy

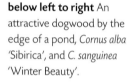

below left to right An attractive dogwood by the edge of a pond, *Cornus alba* 'Sibirica', and *C. sanguinea* 'Winter Beauty'.

Cotoneaster

Grow cotoneasters to provide a show of berries from autumn into winter, which range in colour from bright, shiny red (*C. adpressus, C. salicifolius* 'Herbstfeur' and *C. conspicuus*) to flashy yellow (*C. frigidus* 'Fructu Luteo'). One of the best is *C. horizontalis* with its spreading, horizontal branches, and the red berries clearly hung along them. They come in all sizes, from tiny shrubs to large trees. You can use the smallest in rockeries, to edge paths or beds and you will get, with the right choice, evergreen leaves, typically white or pink flowers (the earliest appearing in spring), and best of all, the berries. Tiny *C. procumbens* practically hugs the ground, *C. adpressus* 'Little Gem' is about 5cm (2in) high, and *C. dammeri* is 15cm (6in) high. *C. astrophoros* is slightly taller at 45cm (18in) and spreads 60–90cm (2–3ft), but takes about 30 years to do so. Good choices for hedges include the red-fruiting *C. glacialis, C. turbinatus* and *C. lacteus*. They can be pruned, and the show of flowers and berries will not suffer.

Height To 5m (15ft)

Flowering time Spring to summer (autumn and winter berries)

Hardiness Fully hardy

Daphne

Evergreen, semi-evergreen or deciduous, these delightful shrubs bear flowers with an exquisite fragrance. Some are rock garden plants, others work well in mixed or shrub borders. Winter-flowering types are best sited near a door where their fragrance can be appreciated to the full without the need to go too far outdoors. *D. bholua* is a borderline hardy, semi-evergreen species that bears deliciously scented clusters of pink and white flowers in late winter. The deciduous and hardiest variety *D. bholua* var. *glacialis* 'Gurkha' bears purplish-pink flowers from mid- to late winter. 'Jacqueline Postill' is evergreen, borderline hardy and has deep purplish-pink flowers. *D. mezereum* is a deciduous species, which suits a woodland garden, and produces reddish, highly scented flowers in late winter. The red summer berries are poisonous, but attractive. *D. tangutica* is a small, evergreen species originating from western China. The fragrant white flowers, which are tinged with rose-purple, appear in late winter to early spring.

Flowering height 60cm–3m (2–10ft)

Flowering time Winter and spring

Hardiness Half-hardy to fully hardy

above left to right *Daphne bholua*, the pretty yellow and dark pink flowers of *Chimonanthus praecox*, and *D. bholua* 'Jacqueline Postill'.

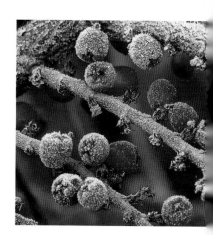

above The bright red berries of *Cotoneaster frigidus* 'Cornubia'.

above left to right
Erica carnea 'Rotes Juwel',
E. x *darleyensis* and *E. carnea.*

below *Erica* x *darleyensis*
'Silberschmelze'.

Erica x darleyensis

Often known as Darley heath, or Darley Dale heath, *Erica* x *darleyensis* has many easy-to-grow hybrids with coloured young foliage and a long flowering period, usually from midwinter (sometimes earlier) until well into spring. The following selection of cultivars are all hardy. 'Archie Graham' has lilac-pink flowers. 'Arthur Johnson' (syn. 'Dunwood Splendour') has pink flowers, which deepen to lilac-pink, and foliage tipped with cream in spring. 'Jack H. Brummage' has lilac-pink flowers and foliage that is yellow-orange throughout the year. 'Jenny Porter' has pinkish-white flowers and cream-tipped foliage. 'Kramer's Rote' has magenta flowers and bronze-tinged foliage. 'Silberschmelze' (syn. 'Molten Silver') has ash-white flowers and foliage faintly tipped with cream in spring. 'White Perfection' has pure white flowers. Unlike most heathers, the Darley heath will tolerate alkaline soil, as long as it is free-draining, and in an open sunny position. By grouping a number of different coloured forms together you can create an effect similar to a multi-coloured patchwork quilt. This is invariably far more interesting and effective than when one or two ericas are grown alone. To add extra height, and prevent the look being too uniform, plant a couple of tall, narrow vertical conifers.

Flowering height To 60cm (24in)
Flowering time Winter to early spring
Hardiness Fully hardy

Garrya elliptica

It makes a remarkably indestructible and attractive evergreen shrub on free-draining soil. It is at its best from midwinter to early spring when it is covered by a mass of dangling grey-green catkins, 15–20cm (6–8in) long. If you want even longer catkins, choose 'James Roof'. *Garrya elliptica* can also be grown as a dense bushy hedge, but should only be pruned and kept in shape once the display of catkins has finished. It grows well in seaside gardens, but does not make a windbreak because it needs a sheltered position. When exposed to a flaying wind, it suffers badly.

Flowering height 4m (12ft)
Flowering time Midwinter to early spring
Hardiness Frost hardy

Hamamelis

The witch hazel genus contains some of the finest winter-flowering shrubs, which would no doubt be more widely grown were it not for their specific cultivation needs. Propagation is also difficult, and plants are slow-growing, so those offered for sale

tend to be small and expensive. Besides their spidery, scented winter flowers, they also have outstanding autumn and winter leaf colour. *H. x intermedia* is a group of variable hybrids. Selections include 'Arnold Promise', which has bright yellow winter flowers and splendid autumn leaf colour; 'Diane' which has red flowers and rich autumn tints; and the rare 'Vesna' with pale copper-coloured flowers and superb autumn leaf colour. *H. mollis*, Chinese witch hazel, is one of the best of the witch hazels. This slow-growing species has scented yellow flowers in midwinter.
Flowering height 4m (12ft)
Flowering time Winter
Hardiness Fully hardy

Jasminum nudiflorum

The winter jasmine has no scent, although the brilliant yellow flowers are undoubtedly welcome in the depths of winter. Not strictly climbing, the stems of this Chinese species are lax and trailing. It can be trained against a wall or allowed to cascade down a bank. The cheery, bright yellow flowers open during warm spells on the bare branches over winter.
Height 2m (7ft) or more
Flowering time Winter and early spring
Hardiness Fully hardy

above left to right
Hamamelis mollis 'Pallida', *Jasminum nudiflorum*, and *H. mollis* 'Pallida' with flowering *Erica carnea* 'Springwood White'.

left Catkins of *Garrya elliptica* in the snow.

above A brightly variegated holly adding extra flashes of colour.

clockwise from top left
Ilex x aquipernyi 'Dragon Lady', *Ilex aquifolium* 'Rubricaulis Aurea', *I. aquifolium* 'Harpune' and *Lonicera fragrantissima*.

Ilex

Hollies are essential in the winter garden. They have three important features. First, the often glossy foliage, sometimes variegated as in the case of *I. aquifolium* 'Argentea Marginata Pendula', *I. aquifolium* 'Golden van Tol' and *I. a.* 'Silver Queen'. The leaves really stand out in the depths of winter, especially when the variegation is bright yellow, as with 'Golden van Tol'. Second, most hollies can be topiarized. Their leaves are quite large so it is hard to convert them into tight-angled shapes, but they will make good lollipops. And third, many have an excellent display of red and yellow berries over winter. Note that if you do want berries you must grow a male and a female in close proximity and check carefully before you buy.

I. x altaclerensis

The Highclere holly is fast-growing and can be clipped to create a hedge, although left unpruned it will make an upright tree, to 20m (65ft) tall. Several attractive cultivars have been developed. The heights and spread vary according to how regularly and closely plants are pruned. 'Belgica Aurea', a compact female form, has leaves that are irregularly edged with yellow; 'Cameliifolia', a female form, which is good for hedging, has glossy, dark green leaves that have smooth edges and turn bronze in cold weather and scarlet berries; 'Golden King', a compact female form, has gold-edged leaves and red berries; 'Lawsoniana', a compact female form, has green leaves with yellow-splashed centres and red berries; and 'Wilsonii', a vigorous female form, has bright green leaves and many bright red berries.
Flowering height To 20m (65ft)
Flowering time Winter berries
Hardiness Fully hardy

I. aquifolium

The common or English holly will also make an upright, large tree if left unchecked, but plants can be pruned and clipped to keep them within bounds.

Some of the cultivars that have been developed have strikingly variegated foliage. 'Argentea Marginata Pendula' (syn. 'Argentea Pendula'), a female form, has cream-edged leaves, purplish stems and red berries; 'Ferox Argentea' (silver hedgehog holly), a slow-growing male form, has sharply spiny, cream-edged leaves; 'Golden Queen' (syn. 'Aurea Regina'), a male form, has spiny, gold-edged leaves; 'Handsworth New Silver', a female form, has purple stems, spiny, cream-edged leaves and bright red berries; 'J.C. van Tol', a self-fertile, female form, has dark green leaves with very few spines and dark red berries; and 'Silver Queen' (syn. 'Silver King'), a slow-growing male form, has cream-edged, spiny leaves.
Flowering height 20m (65ft)
Flowering time Winter berries
Hardiness Fully hardy

I. crenata

The Japanese or box-leaved holly has small, dark green, glossy leaves. It can be clipped to form good topiary shapes and produces black or, sometimes, white or yellow berries. 'Golden Gem', a spreading, compact, female form, has yellow-flecked leaves and black berries.
Flowering height 5m (15ft)
Flowering time Winter berries
Hardiness Fully hardy

Lonicera fragrantissima

A good plant for winter interest, this deciduous or semi-evergreen Chinese honeysuckle species has small, fragrant, white and pink flowers in midwinter. It keeps flowering from the time the leaves fall in autumn until early spring. Unfortunately, it is rather dull the rest of the time, unless used as a support for annual climbers, such as sweet peas. Nonetheless, it is a vital plant for winter gardens.
Flowering height 1.5m (5ft)
Flowering time Winter and early spring
Hardiness Fully hardy

above *Viburnum* x *bodnantense.*

below left to right
Mahonia trifolia, M. x *media* 'Buckland' in full flower, and *M.* x *media* 'Lionel Fortescue'.

Mahonia

The genus contains about 70 species of evergreen shrubs, which are rather similar to *Berberis* – in fact, some botanists would like to unite the genera. Most have deliciously scented flowers, but their prime use is to fill inhospitable sites.

M. aquifolium

Mountain grape holly or Oregon grape, as it is commonly known, has glossy green leaves and racemes of yellow flowers in late winter to early spring. There are a number of cultivars, including the vigorous and low-growing 'Apollo', and 'Smaragd', which has bronze, netted foliage.
Flowering height 1m (3ft)
Flowering time Late winter and spring
Hardiness Fully hardy

M. japonica

This erect species produces arching racemes of scented yellow flowers from early winter to early spring, followed by blue-purple berries. The selection 'Bealei' has more compact flower spikes.
Flowering height 2m (7ft)
Flowering time Winter to spring
Hardiness Fully hardy

M. lomariifolia

This elegant species is one of the parents of *M.* x *media* (the other is *M. japonica*), which it resembles in some respects, though it is more rangy in habit and slightly less resistant to extreme cold. The racemes of flowers, which smell like lily-of-the-valley, appear from late autumn to winter and are followed by bluish, grape-like fruits.
Flowering height 3m (10ft)
Flowering time Late autumn to winter
Hardiness Fully hardy

M. x media

This hybrid group includes a number of notable named garden selections, all similar and equally effective and all with long racemes of fragrant yellow flowers in winter. Leggy specimens can be pruned hard in spring. They include 'Charity', which has slender, upright, spreading spikes of very fragrant yellow flowers; 'Lionel Fortescue', which has upright plumes of bright yellow, slightly less fragrant flowers; and 'Winter Sun', which has dense clusters of bright yellow flowers.
Flowering height To 5m (15ft)
Flowering time Late autumn to late winter
Hardiness Fully hardy

M. trifolia

This unusual species is variable, existing in both prostrate and more upright forms. The short spikes of yellow flowers appear in spring, and the leaves flush purple-red in cold weather.

Flowering height 2m (7ft)
Flowering time Late winter and spring
Hardiness Fully hardy

Sarcococca

Christmas box, or sweet box, are excellent plants for the winter garden and have small but highly scented flowers among the shiny evergreen leaves. Use them with snowdrops, *Arum italicum* subsp. *italicum* 'Marmoratun' and early hellebores. They make excellent groundcover under deciduous trees, and flowering stems can be cut for use in winter flower arrangements. *S. confusa* is a low-growing shrub with glossy, dark green leaves. In winter it produces clusters of fragrant white flowers, and these are followed by glossy black fruits. The naturally occurring variety *S. hookeriana* var. *digyna*, the most widely grown form, has equally fragrant white flowers with pink sepals in mid- to late winter and blackish-blue fruit. *S. humilis* is a dwarf shrub, bearing pink-tinged, white flowers and blackish-blue fruit.

Flowering height To 1.5m (5ft)
Flowering time Winter
Hardiness Fully hardy

Viburnum

This large and important genus consists of both evergreen and deciduous shrubs that, between them, provide interest throughout the year. Some are grown for their flowers (winter or spring), others for their berries, and some for both. They are essential plants. Native species are excellent in wild gardens, providing food for birds in winter. Others are good in winter gardens or mixed borders. A select few make good specimens. *V. tinus*, which can be trained as a standard, is an important evergreen winter shrub. It has a rounded habit and white flowers in late winter or early spring. Bluish-black berries follow the flowers. The flowers of the popular cultivar 'Eve Price' open from rich eye-catching pink buds. *V.* x *bodnantense* 'Dawn' is one of the stars of the winter garden. It is a highly desirable upright, deciduous, vase-shaped shrub with richly scented, pink flowers opening in mild spells from autumn to spring. *V. plicatum* f. *tomentosum* produces blue-black berries in autumn and winter as the leaves redden. *V. farreri* (syn. *V. fragrans*) is deciduous, but it provides a major attraction in late autumn and early winter with its pretty, scented white flowers. The flowers are followed by a good show of tiny, round bright berries. It grows to a height of about 3m (10ft).

Flowering height To 3m (10ft)
Flowering time Late autumn to spring
Hardiness Fully hardy

above left to right
Vibernum tinus 'Eve Price', *Sarcococca confusa* and *Viburnum plicatum* 'Mariesii'.

below *Viburnum tinus* 'Gwenllian'.

trees

The forms of trees are seen at their best in winter when many perennials and bulbs are taking a rest. They come in all shapes and sizes, from the pencil-thin, which shoot straight up, to giants for large gardens. The best have coloured bark, ranging from white to shiny brown, from green to a marbling of white with grey and fawn. Some have twisty, curly stems, which form patterns against the sky. There are also plenty of trees for medium-sized gardens, many offering an excellent show of autumn and winter berries.

Betula

Birches are among the best garden trees. They are hardy and easy to grow in addition to being graceful and quick growing. Most have attractive, usually white bark and good autumn leaf colour. They are among the most reliable trees for alkaline soils. *B. utilis* var. *jacquemontii* is a naturally occurring variety of the Himalayan birch, which has white bark, making it an outstanding plant for the winter garden. The oval leaves turn yellow in autumn. Many of the plants sold in the trade under this name are raised from seed collected in the Himalayas, so habits and growth rates can vary, but most will not exceed a height of 12m (40ft) in 20 years. Selected seedlings include 'Grayswood Ghost', which has glossy leaves; the fast-growing 'Jermyns', which has rounded leaves and large catkins (pussy willows); and 'Silver Shadow', which has large, drooping, dark green leaves. All three forms have particularly brilliant bark.

Height To 25m (82ft)

Flowering time Spring (autumn foliage, winter bark)

Hardiness Fully hardy

Corylus

Hazels provide long, dangly yellow catkins from late winter to early spring. The best form of hazel to buy is undoubtedly *C. avellana* 'Contorta', known as the corkscrew hazel or sometimes called Harry Lauder's walking stick. What makes it so special is the array of zig-zagging, twisty stems that really stand out in the winter, after the leaves have dropped. The stems can be used in cut flower displays. When you cut several stems for an indoor flower arrangement, hammer the stems well before giving them a long drink. As well as their striking stems, they have a fantastic array of twisty, thin, corkscrewing bare branches. They make a lively architectural tracery against the sky. *Corylus* grows well in most soils but they must be free-draining and fertile. A pruning regime is not necessary, but if you want to thin out the tangle of stems or prune to restrict size, do so over winter from the end of autumn to the start of spring.

Height 5m (15ft)
Flowering time Late winter
Hardiness Fully hardy

Eucalyptus

A familiar sight in many urban areas, eucalyptus trees are often planted as pollution-tolerant street trees. Not all species are fully hardy. Although potentially very large, they respond well to pruning. The foliage of most species changes shape as the tree matures, the juvenile leaves being generally considered the more attractive. Cutting back stems or pollarding regularly ensures that trees retain their youthful appearance. *E. pauciflora* subsp. *niphophila*, commonly known as snow gum or alpine snow gum, is a slow-growing evergreen tree, grown for its brilliant, peeling, cream and grey bark. It is shown to best advantage when the plant is grown as a multi-stemmed tree. The bluish-grey juvenile leaves are oval; adult leaves are sickle-shaped. It is hardier than many types of eucalyptus and will grow in any well-drained soil in full sun. It has the most beautiful bark, and is well worth growing.

Height 6m (20ft) or more
Flowering time Late spring to summer (winter bark)
Hardiness Fully hardy to frost tender

below left to right
Corylus avellana 'Contorta', *C. avellana* with catkins in winter and *Eucalyptus pauciflora* subsp. *niphophila*.

Prunus

The ornamental cherries are usually regarded as spring-flowering species, but there are two trees that ought to be in every winter garden. They are *P. serrula* and *P.* x *subhirtella* 'Autumnalis'. The former offers striking, shiny bark, with white flowers in the spring making a beautiful combination, followed by fruit resembling cherries. The latter has an intermittent show of flowers, which starts in the autumn. They are not big but they are abundant.

below left to right
There is room for the shiny, brown-stemmed *Prunus serrula* even in medium-sized gardens – grow it as a feature plant where it can be clearly seen; *Prunus serrula* planted with *Viburnum tinus,* and *Prunus* x *subhirtella* 'Autumnalis'.

P. serrula

A Tibetan cherry tree from western China, this is usually planted for its gleaming, mahogany-red bark, which peels off in strips to produce an eye-catching feature in winter. Site it where the tree will be well lit by the winter sun.
Height 10m (33ft)
Flowering time Spring (winter bark)
Hardiness Fully hardy

P. x subhirtella 'Autumnalis'

The autumn cherry, which was developed in Japan, is probably the finest winter-flowering tree, producing flushes of pink-tinged, white flowers throughout winter during mild spells. The peak display usually occurs right at the end of winter, shortly before the equinox. The leaves turn yellow in autumn.
Height 8m (25ft)
Flowering time Winter
Hardiness Fully hardy

Stewartia pseudocamellia

The peeling pink to red-brown and grey bark of this deciduous tree is a distinctive feature in the winter. The finely toothed, dark green leaves turn yellow to orange to red during the autumn. Cup-shaped, white flowers are borne singly or in pairs in midsummer.
Height 20m (65ft)
Flowering time Midsummer (winter bark)
Hardiness Fully hardy

Salix

The willow genus contains creeping shrubs as well as some quite large trees. Willows offer a variety of attractions for the garden. Many are grown for their catkins (pussy willows) or brightly coloured young shoots – regular annual or biennial hard pruning ensures a good supply – and weeping varieties look attractive growing at the water's edge. *S. babylonica* var. *pekinensis* 'Tortuosa' is a bizarre tree almost grown exclusively for the interest of its twisted stems, at their most striking in winter. *S. caprea* 'Kilmarnock' is a weeping miniature, with cascades of silver-white catkins in late winter. The tree is created artificially by grafting a prostrate plant on to rootstocks of varying height. *S. x sepulcralis* var. *chrysocoma* is a fast-growing golden weeping willow that is possibly the most familiar of all willows. It is an evocative sight when the tips of its arching branches trail in water. It is equally attractive when bare in winter as when it is clothed in its bright green, lance-shaped leaves in summer.

Height To 15m (50ft)
Flowering time Spring (winter stems)
Hardiness Fully hardy

Tilia

Many forms of lime tree make excellent garden plants. Pollard or pleach them to restrict their size, albeit at the expense of the flowers. Lime trees will grow in any moderately fertile, well-drained soil (preferably alkaline), in sun or light shade. *T. cordata*, small-leaved lime, is an upright European species that flowers in midsummer; the heart-shaped leaves turn yellow in autumn. *T. c.* 'Winter Orange' is a desirable selection, with golden-orange young stems that are a feature in winter. Cut back hard for the best winter display. The leaves of *T. platyphyllus* 'Rubra' turn yellow in autumn, and shoots are red in winter.

Height 25m (82ft) (unpollarded)
Flowering time Midsummer (winter stems)
Hardiness Fully hardy

below left to right
The bark of *Stewartia pseudocamellia* in winter, *Tilia platyphyllus,* and *Salix babylonica* var. *pekinensis* 'Tortuosa'.

conifers

above *Abies procera.*

Conifers offer a fantastic range of colours and shapes, from giant specimens like the Leyland cypress to prostrate dwarfs that hug the ground. There are hundreds to choose from. Most are evergreen, and they inject an enormous amount of interest to the winter garden. By themselves some might not look spectacular, but they come into their own when they are planted as focal points, in combination with each other or in association with winter-flowering heathers. For the best range, visit a nursery specializing in conifers.

Abies

Silver firs are found throughout Europe, North Africa, Asia and North America, especially in mountainous areas. Many grow too large for the average garden, but there are some dwarf and slow-growing forms. The compact forms can be planted in borders and rock gardens, although some of the larger species look best when grown as feature plants. Most silver firs are conical and all are evergreen. Grow them in well-drained, slightly acid soil.

below left to right *Abies cephalonica,* cones of *A. koreana* and *A. amabilis.*

A. amabilis

The Pacific silver fir is not widely grown, but the selection 'Spreading Star' makes excellent groundcover. The glossy, dark green needles smell of oranges when they are crushed, and the cones are deep purple.
Height 50cm (20in)
Hardiness Fully hardy

A. balsamea

Balsam fir, or balm of Gilead, is unfamiliar in gardens, but it has a number of notable cultivars. All are hardy. Those classified as Hudsonia Group are dwarf trees, usually compact and rounded in form, although there is some variation. 'Nana', a good rock garden conifer, makes a dome-shaped bush, which is tolerant of some shade. The aromatic, shiny green, needle-like leaves, shorter than those on the species, are arranged in two ranks on the stems; the cones are purplish-blue.
Height To 15m (50ft)
Hardiness Fully hardy

A. cephalonica

Greek fir is a rare tree and, at 30m (100ft) in height, it is unsuitable for small gardens, but the selection

'Meyer's Dwarf' (syn. 'Nana') is more manageable at a height of 50cm (20in), forming a low, spreading, flat-topped, shade-tolerant mound that is good in a rock garden. The needle-like leaves are glossy green and are shorter than on the species; the cones are greenish-brown and resinous.
Height To 30m (100ft)
Hardiness Fully hardy

A. koreana

Korean fir is one of the most attractive of the silver firs. It is notable for its impressive violet cones, which age to brown. The needles are dark green.
Height 10m (33ft)
Hardiness Fully hardy

A. procera

Noble fir (syn. *A. nobilis*), from the western United States, forms a cone-shaped tree, which matures to a broader, irregular obelisk. The greyish-green needles, sometimes with a bluish cast, are arranged in two ranks. Mature trees have silvery-grey, fissured bark; the cones are green. The noble fir makes an attractive specimen, particularly when young; it is sometimes used as a Christmas tree. It is wind-tolerant and reliable at high altitudes.
Height To 45m (150ft)
Hardiness Fully hardy

Cedrus

This is a small genus of only four species, but arguably it contains the most magnificent of all conifers when mature. They are generally suitable only for large gardens, but they are worth considering if you are prepared to remove them once they start to get too large. They make ideal lawn specimens if they can be allowed the space to grow to maturity.

C. atlantica

Originating from the Atlas Mountains in North Africa, this species is less common in gardens than some of the following selections. 'Aurea' has bright, golden-yellow leaves. *C. atlantica* f. *glauca* ('Blue Atlas' cedar) is one of the most handsome forms. Initially cone-shaped, it develops a more spreading crown. The needles, white when young but becoming bright glaucous blue, are arranged in clusters; the cones are light green. Plants in cultivation are normally sold under the name Glauca Group (indicating that they may vary). 'Glauca Pendula', also glaucous blue, has an arching leader and pendulous branches, and it develops as a tent-like structure. It can be kept small by cutting back the central leader, which will persuade the horizontal branches to spread more widely (they may need support as a result).
Height 40m (130ft)
Hardiness Fully hardy

above left to right *Cedrus atlantica* 'Aurea', *C. atlantica* 'Glauca Pendula', and *C. a.* f. *glauca* 'Blue Atlas'.

below *Abies balsamea* 'Nana' is compact in form and ideal for rock gardens.

Chamaecyparis

False cypress is a useful genus, from East Asia and North America, with a huge number of cultivars. They range from giant forest trees to smaller forms that can be used as specimen trees, for hedging and as dwarf plants for the rock or scree garden.

C. lawsoniana

Lawson cypress (syn. *Cupressus lawsoniana*), a conical tree, native to North America, is too large for many gardens, but it has given rise to many cultivars of widely diverging habits. All are hardy. Among the best dwarfs is 'Aurea Densa', which is rounded and one of the outstanding golden-leaved cultivars. It grows to 2m (7ft). The slow-growing 'Bleu Nantais' is another good blue-green, making a cone-shaped mound, about 1.5m (5ft) high. Both have needle-like leaves that become scale-like. Taller varieties include the conical 'Ellwoodii', which is one of the most popular grey-green varieties. The weeping 'Pembury Blue' has striking bluish-grey foliage.
Height To 15m (50ft)
Hardiness Fully hardy

C. obtusa

Hinoki cypress (syn. *Cupressus obtusa*) is less tolerant of lime than some species, and it is not widely planted, yielding to its many cultivars. 'Crippsii' (syn. 'Crippsii Aurea') is a rich gold when grown in full sun, making a fine specimen reaching 15m (50ft). 'Nana Gracilis' is a dwarf cultivar, forming a rough pyramid.
Height To 20m (65ft)
Hardiness Fully hardy

x Cupressocyparis

The value of this much maligned hybrid genus between *Chamaecyparis nootkatensis* and *Cupressus macrocarpa* lies in the trees' speed of growth. It is often planted as hedging where a pollution-resistant screen is needed quickly, and it makes a tough, tight hedge, but only if cut regularly. Allowed to grow freely, it gets out of hand.

opposite from top, left to right x *Cupressocyparis leylandii* 'Leighton Green', x *C. leylandii* 'Golconda' and *Cupressus arizonica* var. *glabra*, *Chamaecyparis lawsoniana* 'Bleu Nantais', *Cupressus arizonica* var. *glabra* 'Blue Ice' and *Chamaecyparis pisifera* 'Filifera Aurea', *Cupressus macrocarpa* 'Donard Gold', *Chamaecyparis lawsoniana* 'Aurea Densa' and *Chamaecyparis obtusa* 'Nana Gracilis'.

x Cupressocyparis leylandii

Leyland cypress is the hybrid mostly used for hedging. All are hardy. 'Golconda', one of the most decorative, forms a narrow cone shape. The scale-like leaves, carried in flattened sprays, are brilliant golden-yellow; the cones are rounded. It is tolerant of clipping. 'Leighton Green' develops as a tall, cone-shaped tree with bright green foliage.
Height To 35m (115ft)
Hardiness Fully hardy

Cupressus

Cypress trees are characteristic of the Mediterranean and are among the stateliest of conifers. They are not always easy to grow away from their native habitat, but they can be used as fine specimens or for hedging. They resent transplanting, so always look for young specimens rather than mature trees.

C. arizonica var. glabra

Smooth cypress (syn. *C. glabra*), which is native to the South-western United States, is a good specimen where space is limited. It forms a regular cone shape. On young specimens the bark is smooth, reddish-purple and flaking; it thickens and turns to greyish-brown on older trees. The scale-like leaves are glaucous bluish-grey and aromatic; the cones are dark brown.
Height To 15m (50ft)
Hardiness Fully hardy

C. macrocarpa

Monterey cypress was once widely used for hedging, but it has largely been superseded by x *Cupressocyparis leylandii*. Excellent cultivars have been developed from the species, however. Both those listed here are borderline hardy. 'Donard Gold' forms an elegant obelisk that gradually becomes conical. The bright yellowish-green leaves are aromatic when crushed. 'Goldcrest' is a desirable smaller version.
Height To 30m (100ft)
Hardiness Mostly fully hardy

above Winter berries on a juniper tree.

below left to right
Juniperus communis 'Hibernica', *Pinus sylvestris* and *Juniperus chinensis* 'Aurea'.

Juniperus

Junipers are usually represented in gardens by the cultivars and hybrids rather than by the species. Many are rock garden plants, while others look good grouped in island beds. They also do well in troughs and containers. Female plants bear berry-like fruits, which may be used to flavour game dishes.

J. chinensis

Chinese juniper is not notable in itself, but it has given rise to many attractive cultivars. 'Aurea' (Young's golden juniper), a slow-growing male selection that forms a narrow obelisk, has aromatic, dull golden-yellow leaves, which are wedge-shaped initially but become scale-like as they mature. Many cones appear in spring, and the tree produces its best colour in sun.
Height To 20m (65ft)
Hardiness Fully hardy

J. communis

Common juniper is found throughout the northern hemisphere. Selections include 'Hibernica' (Irish juniper), which makes a distinctive, narrow shrub, the foliage having a bluish-green cast. The range of cultivars also includes the dwarf, slow-growing kind, though they will eventually, after many years, reach 9m (30ft). Note that some plants are male and some female. The latter are well worth growing because they have round green berries with a greyish tinge, which eventually end up black, though this takes from two to three years.
Height 3–5m (10–15ft)
Hardiness Fully hardy

J. horizontalis

Creeping juniper is a ground-hugging conifer from North America. The species forms a mat of greyish-green leaves, which are needle-like when young, becoming scale-like with age, with dark blue berries. There are many attractive cultivars, all suitable for groundcover. 'Blue Chip' (syn. 'Blue Moon') has glaucous blue foliage. 'Douglasii' is bluish-green, turning rich purple in autumn. 'Golden Carpet' is bright yellowish-green.
Height To 30cm (12in)
Hardiness Fully hardy

Picea

Spruces are found throughout the northern hemisphere and are widely planted as Christmas trees, *P. abies* being the usual choice. There is a wide range of garden varieties, some with grey, yellow or blue foliage. Most are symmetrical in shape, and there are many dwarf forms suitable for rock gardens.

P. abies

The Norway spruce is native to Scandinavia, and is a conical tree. It is the traditional choice for Christmas trees in Europe. 'Gregoryana' is an attractive dwarf selection that makes an impenetrable mound of dark green foliage. It is one of the most compact of all dwarf conifers, growing to about 60cm (2ft).
Height To 40m (130ft)
Hardiness Fully hardy

P. pungens

The Colorado spruce is the parent of many notable garden plants. 'Globosa', which forms a neat dome or mound, has bristle-like, glaucous green foliage, arranged radially. 'Montgomery' is silver-blue, making a broad-based cone. Slow-growing, it should be among the first choices for a specimen tree in a small garden.
Height To 15m (50ft)
Hardiness Fully hardy

Pinus

Most pines, such as *Pinus sylvestris*, are unsuitable as garden plants, magnificent though they are, since they are nearly all too large for the average plot. Selection by nurserymen has produced a number of useful clones that are more manageable, however. The needles, which are sometimes quite long, are held in characteristic bundles.

P. mugo

Dwarf mountain pine is a useful conifer from central Europe that is less widely grown than its many garden-worthy clones, many of them dwarf and ideal for a rock garden. 'Corley's Mat' makes a prostrate, spreading carpet. The slow-growing 'Mops' is almost spherical with resinous brown buds in winter.
Height 3.5m (11ft)
Hardiness Fully hardy

above A close-up of the bright blue-tinged needles of *Picea pungens* 'Hoopsii'.

below left to right
Picea pungens 'Montgomery', *Pinus mugo* 'Corley's Mat' and *Picea abies* 'Gregoryana'.

WINTER DISPLAYS

Planning a garden that looks attractive and interesting in winter requires some thought. There are plenty of plants that will provide colour, form and fragrance in the winter garden, but it is important to integrate these with the other plants that are grown primarily for their appearance in spring and summer. The winter garden also depends to a large extent on the underlying structure and design for its effect. The bare bones of the hard landscaping and boundaries are more noticeable in winter, and all planting must be planned to enhance the built features when they are most exposed.

left *Galanthus* 'Magnet' has taller, larger flowers than *Galanthus nivalis* (common snowdrop). Here, it forms a marvellous carpet beneath the witch hazel *Hamamelis* x *intermedia* 'Pallida'.

carpets of colour

The best way to make sure that the winter garden looks good is to work in layers from the bottom up. Start off with small plants that hug the ground, then make sure you have interesting shapes in beds and borders over the winter months, before moving on to topiary, trees, conifers, and artificial shapes.

winter bulbs

Many people think that the only bulbs worth planting are those that flower in spring, yet there are some sensational ones for the winter. These will brighten up a woodland garden or a patch of ground beneath a deciduous tree. This is an ideal place for planting because the bare branches mean that bright light reaches the ground in winter, when the bulbs need it most. The trees are also dormant now, taking up less moisture from the ground. Conversely, in summer, when the bulbs are taking a rest and not needing too much moisture, the trees are in full growth. The two make a perfect combination.

The pick of the bulbs includes *Cyclamen coum*, *Eranthis hyemalis* (winter aconite) and *Galanthus* (snowdrop). Cyclamen should be planted in big, bold groups for the best effect. Because they are so small, just 5–7.5cm (2–3in) high, a single plant can easily get lost, but together their beautifully patterned leaves really stand out. Some are completely green and some have silver marbling. Their shapes vary from round to kidney-shaped. In the wild they grow in shady mountain sites, invariably with good drainage, and the two key qualities they need in the garden are summer shade and gritty, free-draining soil. In the right conditions just a few plants will eventually create a wonderful spread.

Winter aconites also do best in open areas under deciduous trees as long as they are well watered (it is vital that they do not bake in the summer). In a mild winter they might start flowering quite early, but generally it takes a good while before the flashy spreads of bright yellow flowers appear. The latter open only in full sun and will not perform in the shade, so do not hide them away. In very bad winters they might not flower until the first days of spring, but the wait is well worth it, especially after a couple of years of planting when they have self-seeded and created an eye-catching show.

Snowdrops are equally showy. There are many kinds with minuscule differences. Choose a sturdy, strong growing cultivar, such as the scented 'S. Arnott' or 'Atkinsii'. They need winter moisture and summer shade so that they do not bake. They soon spread, making great swathes of white. Some make lovely cut flowers for any indoor display.

above Pretty snowdrops always provide a bright white show.

below The best place to grow *Cyclamen coum* is around the base of a large, deciduous tree.

above A frosty, wintry scene embellished by the upstanding plumes of *Cortaderia selloana*.

below Well designed round beds, with plants layered in height from the smallest at the front to the tallest.

borders

Before you dig a new border, it is vital that you first decide what its outline will look like in winter, when it is clearly visible and most of the plants are taking a rest. Walk around the garden, getting different views, and decide whether you need a circular shape, a smart triangle, a series of beds with paths weaving between them, or a single, impressive island bed.

It is also important to decide how you are going to edge it. To make the border stand out, you could use treated posts, sawn into lengths, to give the edges a distinctive, rustic look. Alternatively, use brick or if it is a large bed, paving. Make sure that the soil is not completely bare from winter to spring. And odd though it sounds, it does not matter if the growth is alive or dead.

Ornamental grasses are excellent value for money. They provide fresh green spring growth, summer flowers and sometimes reddish-orange autumn colour. It can be very tempting to cut down the dead stems at the start of winter, but do not do so. Leave them. They look especially attractive when rimed with winter frost. They also provide interesting shapes and seedheads. The best time to cut them down is in late winter, before the new spring growth begins.

pampas grass and evergreens

Some of the most sensational ornamental grasses include the pampas grasses. They can grow 3m (10ft) high in the case of the popular *Cortaderia selloana*, which has several, excellent cultivars. 'Sunningdale Silver' has strong, vertical flowering stems, topped by beautiful, silvery-creamy-white plumes. Leave them standing over winter, and the winter garden will be immeasurably enhanced. Structural seedheads left uncut over winter can look stunning in wintry frosts.

There are several low-growing conifers that can be used to provide year-round groundcover, but do not overlook *Hedera* spp. (ivy), which are available in a wide range of leaf colour and shape and which can be easily kept under control by simply pulling up straggling stems. In reliably moist soil and shade the glossy, evergreen leaves of *Pachysandra terminalis* will quickly create a dense mat through which taller spring-flowering bulbs can emerge.

theatrical touches

You do not need a grand garden for a theatrical touch. A stylish flourish can perk up the smallest garden. Make sure that each effect is fully embellished. A statue by itself might be fine, but it will look even more effective against a background of winter evergreens. This can be anything from dwarf evergreen bamboos to smart shrubs and conifers. They will stand out even more beautifully and dramatically when the garden is covered in snow.

above A lively mix of shapes will keep the winter garden alive. Combine verticals (seedheads and trees) with strong horizontals (the hedge top and path running from left to right).

left A stylish feature such as a sundial will look equally attractive in winter and summer.

above Large topiary like this needs a spacious lawn, but the design can easily be scaled down for a more intimate setting.

below and right These well-established pieces of topiary create a wonderful sense of rhythm, leading on the eye to the end of the garden.

topiary

Topiary can be as traditional or as modern, as abstract or representational as you wish. All that counts is that you choose the right plant for cutting, pruning and shaping and that it fits in with the rest of the garden.

boxing clever

For traditional evergreen topiary use *Buxus* (box). It can be used to make all kinds of shapes, from squares to balls and peacocks. The small leaves mean you can create precise shapes with tight angles, and it is quite fast growing, at about 30cm (12in) a year. Box responds well to regular clipping.

You can buy box plants at various heights, some of which are already trained, although they are expensive. Alternatively, buy an unpruned box plant that is about three years old. Plant it where it is needed, and then take your time deciding what shape will look best. You can be as unconventional as you want, creating all kinds of intricate shapes, including cubes with a central stem poking out of the top,

trained into a globe, with a central stem poking out of that, and a small bird trained on top of that.

The simplest shapes are created by eye and require three things – a sharp pair of secateurs, a clear idea of what you want to achieve and a steady hand. If necessary, buy a ready-made, three-dimensional template to stand over the plant, or make a former yourself using chicken wire. It does not matter if the topiary is not exactly as you would wish because further snippings and growth will rectify any mistakes.

Do make sure that whatever you create has room to grow and fill out, with visitors given plenty of space to stand back and appreciate what you have done. Topiary never works when you are standing right on top of it, unable to see how it fits into the rest of the garden. It needs to be seen from a distance.

hedge topiary

The most formal, structural plants in the garden often make the best topiary, and that includes evergreen hedges. Too often they are left as sprawling, misshapen slabs around the garden, when they can so easily be turned into something elegant, beautiful and striking.

Box hedges can be given a battlemented look, a straight top or one with an array of shapes. They include balls and pyramids, at regular intervals, and merely require someone with a head for heights perched on a sturdy stepladder. Make sure that the shapes have sloping or rounded tops, so that snow can easily slide off. It is easy to swish snow off topiary in the garden so that the shapes do not get squashed, but at the top of a hedge that can be extremely tricky.

Other plants for topiary, besides box, include *Ilex* (holly), *Prunus lusitanica* (Portugal laurel) and *Taxus baccata* (common yew). You can also train *Hedera* spp. (ivy) over wire shapes for instant, easy topiary. Just shear all the leaves off one side so that you are faced with an attractive, twisty mass of short, bare stems. Right on top, and down the other side, will be a 7.5cm (3in) layer of leaves. This creates a thin curtain of foliage that filters the light.

The best way to start a beech hedge is by planting bare-root trees over winter, 15–30cm (6–12in) apart. Do this when the weather is clement. Let the beech reach its final height, say 2.5m (8ft), then prune the top growth in late autumn or early winter, as the sap levels fall. At the same time, shear the growth off one side. Old established hedges can be pruned over two or three years, to minimize the shock. Keep cutting off new growth on the bald side.

The effect is highly striking and unusual. It is not traditional topiary, but it is a clever way of manipulating growth to a stylish, surprising effect. The ultimate aim is to keep the winter garden alive, and flourishing. By injecting extra levels of interest, your winter garden will bring as much pleasure as it does in the summer.

above A pair of beautifully shaped cones make a grand statement standing in front of the archway through this hedge.

left This is a particularly bold piece of shapely, striking topiary.

below Small parterres should be placed near a house, where they can be looked down upon.

tree schemes

The importance of trees in garden design can easily be overlooked. In summer they are part of the scene, making masses of leafy growth, but in winter, when the bare branches are revealed, they often have a majestic beauty.

Trees need to be looked after as much as small plants to give their best. The best trees have either coloured stems or create wonderful silhouettes against the light. Mature trees might well need thinning at some stage if they are to be effective. Lopping off branches lets light get to the ground, where there are bulbs, and also makes sure that the tree has an open, striking outline. It is also important to make sure that any twiggy growth sprouting out of the base of the trunk is removed, giving a clean look.

planting trees

When you are planting trees make sure that they fit in with the rest of the scheme. At ground level this might include a sensational spread of a white-flowering *Erica carnea* (winter heath), creating an effect like snow. To this, add rich, glossy, shiny greens, deep purples and variegated yellowish leaves. With just a few choice colours a large part of the garden can be given an astonishing make-over.

It is also important to make sure that trees are integrated by working down from (or up to) their great height. Provide adjacent hedges and shrubs, in different shapes and colours, so that each stratum is clearly visible. The bare-stemmed *Cornus alba* and *C. stolonifera*, and their different cultivars, add a range of blackish-purple, bright red and yellow-green vertical stems that strikingly reach for the sky.

There are also plenty of small trees for medium-sized gardens. The most important thing is that every plant has its own space, and that each ingredient blends without jarring.

opposite The winter garden scene with *Erica carnea* 'Springwood White' on the ground, and a magisterial tree showing where branches have been removed to open up its striking shape.

left The candelabra-effect of a *Prunus* tree set against pyramids and verticals.

below left A deft fusion of foreground green, middle-ground flame-red, and a background mix of the two.

below The coloured stems of a *Cornus* cleverly placed against a lilac background.

above A stylish hedge using alternate green and golden conifers.

conifers

The most important point about a winter garden is that the design and the planting create a strong shape and structure. It is easy to pack a garden with summer-flowering plants, but a one-season wonder is no good whatsoever. Carefully selected and sited conifers are essential ingredients of the well-planned garden.

what do they do?

The best conifers add shapes and contours whether you want a formal or informal scheme. With heights ranging from 1m (3ft) for a dwarf conifer, such as *Picea pungens* 'Globosa', to the 90m (300ft) high *Sequoiadendron giganteum* (giant redwood), there is a conifer for most situations.

Conifers are best appreciated in winter, when the rest of the garden is relatively quiet. Many have decorative cones. Those of *Abies koreana* (Korean fir) are a striking violet-blue, while those of *Pinus peuce* (Macedonian pine) exude white resin. *Pinus bungeana* has decorative bark, richly deserving its common

right A beautifully subtle range of coloured conifers.

name, the lacebark pine. The bark flakes off to reveal creamy patches that darken to purplish grey-green. Some cultivars of *Cryptomeria japonica* (Japanese cedar) that retain their juvenile foliage redden dramatically in winter. And the blue-green leaved conifers are a boon to winter gardens because they develop their most intense leaf colour in cold, frosty weather.

If you have a medium-to-large sized garden, plant tall conifers at the boundary edge. When they are planted within a garden they can take up a huge amount of space and cast considerable shadows behind them.

In a small garden you could create a miniature pinetum using dwarf conifers, including *Pinus mugo* 'Corley's Mat', *Thuja plicata* 'Irish Gold' and *Tsuga canadensis* 'Jeddeloh'. Alternatively, space them around the garden to create a variety of midwinter shapes. Concentrate on extremes, including the round and columnar, especially those like the 5m (15ft) high, 30cm (12in) wide *Juniperus communis* 'Hibernica'.

exciting combinations

Where space permits, try combining and contrasting a number of different shapes. For example, the columnar *Chamaecyparis lawsoniana* 'Green Pillar' goes well with the prostrate junipers *Juniperus procumbens* or *J. squamata* 'Holger'. Others are best as specimen trees in grass or gravel.

In a large garden *Cedrus libani* (cedar of Lebanon) is an automatic first choice for its sensational shape with wide-spreading branches. Equally handsome are its relatives. *Cedrus atlantica* (Atlas cedar) has attractive, fissured bark and a giant height of 40m (130ft). The bark is silver-grey, and the leaves are dark green to greenish-blue. The form 'Aurea' is much slower-growing and has striking bright golden-yellow foliage. *Picea breweriana* (Brewer spruce) and *P. omorika* (Serbian spruce) are also very good choices. The latter has brown bark that cracks into square shapes and leaves tinged with blue.

avenues and dwarfs

Many conifers have special uses. For example, the upright *Taxus baccata* 'Fastigiata' (Irish yew), 5m (15ft) high and 1m (3ft) wide, makes traditional sentry-like shapes to either side of an avenue, framing a vista. You can also try planting dwarf conifers close together so that they grow into each other, assuming a sculptural air. Some form dense mats, particularly *Juniperus horizontalis*, *J. squamata* and *J. procumbens*. Many dwarf conifers are also ideal candidates for rock gardens.

windbreaks

Some conifers make excellent windbreaks. Rapid growers such as x *Cupressocyparis leylandii* grow at 1m (3ft) a year for 20 years, then at 60cm (2ft) a year. Give them space or prune them regularly. Stop them at hedge height, trimming them twice a year, slowing them down and keeping them at about 2m (7ft) high.

above A clever planting scheme showing the range of shapes offered by different, first-rate conifers.

left A collection of large conifers makes a magisterial statement in the depths of winter.

above The classically proportioned features of an angel adding a nostalgic garden touch.

above right Metal discs make an unobtrusive and unusual stepping-stone effect down the length of a gravel path.

artificial effects

The range of materials that can be used in a garden includes the old and the new. Both can be used in all kinds of ways, and they must either merge with and enhance the existing look, being dictated by the planting scheme and atmosphere, or wittily stand out, catching visitors by surprise. The best gardens have a touch of both, using a wide range, from stone, shells and water to concrete, metal, plastic, stained glass, coloured pebbles, ornamental tiles, paint, wood, artificial lighting and slide projectors. In short, anything goes, but only if it looks good.

statuary

Antique statues are expensive, but it is now possible to buy modern reproductions of such high quality that it is often hard to tell the difference, especially when yogurt has been smeared over them to encourage the growth of lichen.

Statues can be used as focal points at the end of a vista or wherever there is a quiet part of the garden that needs a dash of grandeur. One grand statue on a plinth in a modest garden will look pompously out of place, but add a couple of smaller, more modest statues, with a face poking out of a border, one behind a pond, or one at the base of a tree, and suddenly you have created the right context for the first statue, and it will look entirely appropriate.

right The perfectly proportioned outline of a statue of a goose waddling across a lawn.

modern materials

Using modern materials in gardens does not mean that they must stand out like eyesores. Rusty metal discs or hub caps can be used to enhance a traditional gravel path, contributing to a rustic look. Replace them with shiny aluminium discs, and the look is lively, upbeat and 21st century. In both cases they inject a sense of movement, especially if the discs are packed close together at the beginning of the path, gradually being spaced further and further apart in the distance to make the path seem longer than it is.

Modern materials can also be used to create a stylish, elegant look. Traditional, high-quality Victorian arbours were incredibly ornate, with intricate wrought-iron patterning, but they can also be bare and minimalist, being used like a picture frame to highlight a topiarized plant. Modern sculptures can be used in witty ways. An elongated, angular face, unlike a rounded classical one, is just the right shape for a grassy, punk-like wig of hair. And the whole effect is softened when other grasses are planted nearby.

a sense of style

If artificial effects begin to dominate the planting, it becomes more of a gallery or playground than a garden. The only time when that does not matter is when you are creating a children's garden.

Although anything goes that gives pleasure, it is usually best to stick to a theme. A path with discs can become a river with stepping stones leading to a monster's lair. Sculptured heads can be given a devilish twist with a coat of paint, giant spiders' webs can be made using lengths of cane, topiarized shrubs may become monsters, and hiding places can be created by close-planting upright shrubs in a semi-circle. If you are artistic, create a mosaic design on a plain wall (perhaps a dull garage) or use oil-based paints to add a *trompe l'oeil* door, apparently opening mysteriously to a secret garden beyond.

above A modern version of an old-fashioned arbour, here used to frame a stylish blue-grey box planter.

left A beautiful, highly inventive combination of a sculptured face with a hollow in the skull for planting a mop of hair-like grass.

pots and tubs

above Evergreen grasses, such as forms of *Festuca*, and bamboos are ideal container plants.

above right This winter-flowering hanging basket contains many evergreen plants, including variegated ivies and *Euphorbia myrsinites*. The blooms of heathers and *Viburnum tinus* add extra interest, but the highlight of the basket is the little *Iris* 'Pauline'.

right The bright yellow flowers of *Eranthis hyemalis* (winter aconite).

When choosing plants for a winter container, see what is available in the garden. There are dozens of small flowering plants at this time of year, and while many are grown under deciduous trees, where they spread freely, many can also be grown in pots to add colour inside the home.

An excellent example is *Eranthis hyemalis* (winter aconite). It has bright yellow flowers offset by highly attractive leaves. You can also grow *Cyclamen coum* or its more tender relative, *C. persicum*. Cyclamen have sweetly-scented pink, red or white flowers through the winter months. Do not keep them in a warm, dry room, however; they need a cool, airy place. This is also the time of year to wander round the garden collecting shapely stems (*Corylus avellana* 'Contorta') and scented flowers (*Hamamelis mollis*) for `display.

window boxes

There are many small plants that can be grown in window boxes and small containers, such as scented hyacinths and hellebores, trailing *Hedera* (ivy), *Ophio-pogon planiscapus* 'Nigrescens', and young phormiums.

Many ivies have leaves that turn an attractive chocolate-brown colour over winter, especially when caught by a frost. They also come in a variety of leaf shapes, from the large to the small and intricate, and many have excellent variegation. The *Ophiopogon* looks like a black-coloured grass, and makes a good contrast with brighter greens. And phormiums, especially *P. tenax* 'Dazzler', have red, orange and pink leaves. Eventually it will get too big for a container and can be planted outside. If it is going from a warm atmosphere to a cold one, make sure that it gradually acclimatizes to its new conditions and provide a deep, dry mulch for winter protection.

above left Hellebores in full flower add plenty of colour just after the winter and into early spring.

above right A stunning combination of young plants for a window box.

left Richly scented, pure white hyacinths look striking in terracotta pots.

WINTER TASKS

A well-planned garden will be packed with colour and interest in the winter months, and working outdoors can be a real pleasure. No matter what the weather, there are always jobs to be done, and tackling them relieves the pressure in spring. Sometimes there is no choice but to become an armchair gardener, however, and this is the time to scan gardening books and plant encyclopedias for ideas to plan minor improvements or to redesign a bed or border or even the whole of your garden, and, of course, to make lists of all those seeds you need to order.

left *Galanthus* 'Atkinsii' early on a frosty winter morning.

early winter

above Service your lawn mower and prepare it for storage over the winter.

The onset of winter inevitably means fewer jobs to do in the garden, but it is a good idea to get outdoors whenever the weather is favourable. There is always tidying-up to be done, and jobs like broken fences to be mended. It makes sense to get work like this finished before the more severe winter weather makes them less appealing. This is an especially good time to take a critical look at how you can improve your soil in time for the next growing season.

Heavy clay soil needs breaking up with horticultural sand and grit and mushroom compost. Fork it in, and smash down thick lumps of soil with the back of a spade, breaking them into pieces. Conversely, poor, thin soil, especially over chalk, will need improving with well-rotted manure. This is demanding work, best done whenever you have time in winter.

above Protect low-growing winter-flowering plants such as *Helleborus niger* from mud and rain damage if you want to cut the blooms for indoors.

plants at their best

- ❖ *Chimonanthus praecox*
- ❖ *Erica carnea*
- ❖ *Erica x darleyensis*
- ❖ *Hamamelis mollis*
- ❖ *Iris unguicularis* (syn. *I. stylosa*)
- ❖ *Ilex*, berries
- ❖ *Jasminum nudiflorum*
- ❖ *Mahonia x media* 'Lionel Fortescue' and 'Charity'
- ❖ *Nerine bowdenii*
- ❖ *Gaultheria*, berries
- ❖ *Prunus x subhirtella* 'Autumnalis'
- ❖ *Pyracantha*, berries
- ❖ *Sarcococca*
- ❖ *Viburnum x bodnantense*
- ❖ *Viburnum farreri*
- ❖ *Viburnum tinus*

above Use pegs and string to mark out a new vegetable bed. Hoe the soil to remove weeds and all their roots, and then dig in plenty of well-rotted organic matter to improve the soil structure.

the flower garden

- ❖ Test your soil
- ❖ Keep weeding when shoots appear
- ❖ Check bulbs, corms and tubers in store
- ❖ Dispose of garden refuse by burning or composting where possible
- ❖ Service your mower or have it done professionally
- ❖ Plant bare-root and balled trees and shrubs
- ❖ Check all bulbs being grown in pots for early flowering
- ❖ Protect vulnerable plants that will remain in the garden
- ❖ Order seeds
- ❖ Take hardwood shrub cuttings
- ❖ Take root cuttings
- ❖ Plant hedges
- ❖ Install a pond heater if you live in a cold area where thick ice is a problem
- ❖ Remove leaves that have fallen on rock plants
- ❖ Cover alpines that need protection from winter wet with a pane of glass
- ❖ Protect flowers of winter plants that might be spoilt by the weather

above If you do not have a cloche, improvise with a piece of polythene (plastic) over wire hoops, or a pane of glass supported on bricks.

the greenhouse and conservatory

❖ Once a week check all plants and pick off any dead or dying leaves before they start to rot
❖ Ventilate on warm days, especially if the greenhouse is well insulated. Poor air circulation can encourage diseases
❖ Except for winter-flowering plants that are still in strong, active growth, gradually give plants less water. Most will then tolerate low temperatures better and diseases should be less of a problem
❖ Put up new shelves and surfaces if required, in readiness for next spring
❖ Check against mice
❖ Buy new pots to replace any that were broken last summer

above Check bulbs and corms in store for any signs of rot. It is worth dusting them with a fungicide suitable for this purpose. Be careful not to inhale any of the dust.

above If you plan to keep your bulbs to grow in the garden, deadhead them as soon as the display is over. This will avoid energy being wasted on seed production.

above Do not plant the bulbs directly into the garden, but acclimatize them gradually in a cold frame or another protected place, such as an unheated greenhouse.

above Plant the bulbs out in a border where they can be left undisturbed.

mid-winter

If you made an early start with winter jobs such as digging and tidying beds and borders, midwinter is mainly a time for indoor jobs including ordering seeds and plants, writing labels and designing improvements for the year ahead. These are not unimportant tasks, and by attending to them in good time you are more likely to make the right decisions and have everything ready for late winter and early spring when gardening begins in earnest.

above Sow seeds for summer flowers. Spread them thinly and as evenly as possible.

the flower garden

❖ Keep an area of water open in an iced-over pond if there is a prolonged freeze. If you don't have a pond heater, try standing a pan of boiling water on the ice until it melts through

❖ Knock heavy snow off hedges and conifers if the branches start to bend under the weight. If you leave it, the shape may be spoilt

❖ Insulate the cold frame for extra protection against the coldest weather

❖ Create new paths, making sure that they are not under deciduous trees where leaves will fall, creating a slippery surface

❖ Create new ponds. Aim for a minimum surface area of 12 sq m (130 sq ft). The more it fills with rain over winter the better, because tap water contains chemicals that lead to the growth of algae in hot summer weather

❖ Use lengths of hosepipe to map out new flower beds, and check that you are happy with the shape. Also make sure that the paths between new beds are wide enough for a wheelbarrow and lawnmower

❖ Avoid walking on wet grass on heavy clay because you will create bumps and dips

above Take chrysanthemum cuttings from a clump of roots that has been overwintered in a greenhouse or cold frame. Choose shoots coming directly from the base of the plant.

above Space the chrysanthemum cuttings evenly around the edge of a pot containing a potting mixture that is suitable for cuttings.

above To take root cuttings, lift a well-established plant to provide the cuttings or remove soil from one side of the parent plant to gain access to the roots.

the greenhouse and conservatory

❖ Once a week check all plants and pick off any dead or dying leaves

❖ Continue ventilating, especially on mild days, but even on cold days for at least 30 minutes. This particularly applies where paraffin heaters are being used because they release small quantities of noxious fumes

❖ Water pot plants, but note that being dormant they only need the occasional drink when dry

❖ Paint plant pots for next spring, jazzing them up with smart blue and white stripes, hothouse reds or low-key pale greys

❖ Clean the greenhouse thoroughly to reduce the build-up of pests and diseases.

above Cold frames of any kind benefit from a warm blanket thrown over them on cold nights. A piece of old carpet is an alternative.

plants at their best

❖ *Calluna vulgaris*
❖ *Cupressus sempervirens*
❖ *Erica* spp.
❖ *Euonymus fortunei* 'Variegatus'
❖ *Garrya elliptica*
❖ *Helleborus* spp.
❖ *Juniperus scopulorum* 'Skyrocket'
❖ *Lonicera* x *purpusii*
❖ *Pinus patula*
❖ *Prunus serrula*
❖ *Rubus cockburnianus*
❖ *Salix babylonica* var. *pekinensis* 'Tortuosa'
❖ *Skimmia japonica* 'Rubella'
❖ *Tilia platyphyllos* 'Rubra'

above Cut each root into pieces about 5cm (2in) long. Fill a pot with gritty potting mixture and insert the cuttings the right way up, using a dibber or pencil to make the hole.

above When planting cuttings of thin roots, you can lay them out horizontally, evenly spaced over a tray of compost, and then cover them with a thin layer of gritty potting mix.

late winter

above Mulching fruit bushes in winter will give them a good start for the rest of the season.

In favourable areas late winter can be almost spring-like, especially in a mild period, but don't be lulled into sowing and planting outdoors too soon. If the weather turns cold, seeds will not germinate, and seedlings and plants may receive such a check to their growth that they do not do as well as those sown or planted later. Concentrate your efforts on indoor sowing, but make the most of frames and cloches, too, for early crops.

One way of getting plants off to an early start (tomatoes and lettuces, for example) is to sow them in small plastic containers, clearly labelled, in a heated greenhouse. This means that when the spring temperatures do pick up, they can be moved outside, under cloches especially at night when the temperatures can suddenly drop. This is also a good time to check the vegetable garden, forking out the roots of perennial weeds. Also continue breaking up heavy lumps on clay soil. If left, the soil will take much longer to heat up in the spring, and the seeds will find it extremely difficult to get off to a flying start.

plants at their best

- ❖ *Crocus tommasinianus*
- ❖ *C. chrysanthus*
- ❖ *Cyclamen coum*
- ❖ *Daphne mezereum*
- ❖ *Eranthis hyemalis*
- ❖ *Erica carnea*
- ❖ *Erica x darleyensis*
- ❖ *Galanthus*
- ❖ *Garrya elliptica*
- ❖ *Helleborus niger*
- ❖ *Helleborus orientalis*
- ❖ *Jasminum nudiflorum*
- ❖ *Iris unguicularis*
- ❖ *Iris reticulata*
- ❖ *Muscari armeniacum*
- ❖ *Narcissus* 'February Gold'
- ❖ *Primula x polyantha*
- ❖ *Prunus cerasifera*
- ❖ *Prunus x subhirtella* 'Autumnalis'

above Take time to tidy up a rock garden, removing any weeds that have taken root and adding fresh chippings.

the flower garden

- ❖ Plant climbers
- ❖ Mulch beds and borders, especially after a night of heavy rain
- ❖ Insulate the cold frame for extra protection against the coldest weather
- ❖ Sow sweet peas
- ❖ Pinch out tips of autumn-sown sweet peas
- ❖ Tidy up the rock garden and apply fresh stone chippings where necessary
- ❖ Check labels on shrubs and border plants and renew if necessary
- ❖ Lay a new lawn from turf, provided the ground is not frozen nor waterlogged

above Many summer bedding plants sown earlier will be ready to prick out into trays.

above Sow early crops in a cold frame if it is not packed with overwintering plants.

above When taking dahlia cuttings, remove a tiny piece of the parent tuber with a shoot and it should root quickly without a rooting hormone.

the greenhouse and conservatory

❖ Take chrysanthemum cuttings
❖ Pot up chrysanthemums rooted earlier
❖ Take dahlia cuttings
❖ Sow seeds of bedding plants and pot plants
❖ Prick out seedlings sown earlier
❖ Increase ventilation on warm days
❖ Make sure the glass is clean so that the plants receive plenty of light
❖ Clean all pots and trays in readiness for saving spring seed
❖ Clean all garden tools, scraping off mud, and oil the wood of spades and forks

above If you have a greenhouse, now is the time to sow seeds of frost-tender plants for summer bedding. Medium-sized seeds are easily scattered using a folded piece of stiff paper.

above If you do not have a propagator, enclose pots or trays of cuttings in a plastic bag. Use sticks or twigs to support the bag so that the leaves do not come into contact with the plastic.

above Plant new container-grown climbers as long as the ground is not frozen or waterlogged. Apply a mulch at least 5cm (2in) around the plant after the ground has been soaked thoroughly.

above Later, prick out the bedding seedlings and space them out evenly in the tray.

GARDENING NOTES

Through trial and error you can create the garden of your dreams, with the certain knowledge that you will have another chance to get it right the next year. Use the following pages to record your successes and failures with existing and new plants to keep as a useful reference for years to come.

left A stunning interplanting of blue agapanthus with *Hemerocallis* (day lily) and pink alliums.

shrubs

above *Viburnum carlesii* 'Diana' produces highly perfumed pink flowers throughout spring.

below *Calluna vulgaris* 'Tib' is excellent in containers and flowers from mid-summer to late autumn.

TYPE ....

Variety..

Pruned ....

Planted ....

Flowered ....

Tip for next year ....

TYPE ....

Variety..

Pruned ....

Planted ....

Flowered..

Tip for next year ....

TYPE ....

Variety..

Pruned ....

Planted ....

Flowered..

Tip for next year ....

TYPE ....

Variety..

Pruned ....

Planted ....

Flowered..

Tip for next year ....

TYPE ....

Variety..

Pruned ....

Planted ....

Flowered..

Tip for next year ....

TYPE ....

Variety..

Pruned ....

Planted ....

Flowered..

Tip for next year ....

TYPE ....

Variety..

Pruned ....

Planted ....

Flowered..

Tip for next year ....

TYPE ....

Variety ....

Pruned ....

Planted ....

Flowered ....

Tip for next year ....

TYPE ....

Variety ....

Pruned ....

Planted ....

Flowered ....

Tip for next year ....

TYPE ....

Variety ....

Pruned ....

Planted ....

Flowered ....

Tip for next year ....

TYPE ....

Variety ....

Pruned ....

Planted ....

Flowered ....

Tip for next year ....

TYPE ....

Variety ....

Pruned ....

Planted ....

Flowered ....

Tip for next year ....

TYPE ....

Variety ....

Pruned ....

Planted ....

Flowered ....

Tip for next year ....

TYPE ....

Variety ....

Pruned ....

Planted ....

Flowered ....

Tip for next year ....

above *Cotinus coggygria* 'Royal Purple' is grown for its striking autumn foliage.

below The brilliantly coloured stems of *Cornus* brighten the winter garden.

bulbs

above *Muscari,* also known as grape hyacinths, are delightful long-flowering spring bulbs.

below Agapanthus grow in eye-catching clumps, and add vivid shades of blue to the summer garden.

TYPE ....   Planted ....

Variety ....   Flowered ....

Tip for next year ....

TYPE ....   Planted ....

Variety ....   Flowered ....

Tip for next year ....

TYPE ....   Planted ....

Variety ....   Flowered ....

Tip for next year ....

TYPE ....   Planted ....

Variety ....   Flowered ....

Tip for next year ....

TYPE ....   Planted ....

Variety ....   Flowered ....

Tip for next year ....

TYPE ....   Planted ....

Variety ....   Flowered ....

Tip for next year ....

TYPE ....   Planted ....

Variety ....   Flowered ....

Tip for next year ....

TYPE .... Planted ....

Variety... Flowered..

Tip for next year ....

TYPE .... Planted ....

Variety... Flowered..

Tip for next year ....

TYPE .... Planted ....

Variety... Flowered..

Tip for next year ....

TYPE .... Planted ....

Variety... Flowered..

Tip for next year ....

TYPE .... Planted ....

Variety... Flowered..

Tip for next year ....

TYPE .... Planted ....

Variety... Flowered..

Tip for next year ....

TYPE .... Planted ....

Variety... Flowered..

Tip for next year ....

above Cyclamen can form carpets of late autumn colour when naturalized under trees.

below Pure white winter snowdrops are perfectly complemented by tiny pink cyclamen.

perennials

above *Primula beesiana* carries small cerise flowerheads on 60cm (2ft) tall stems.

below Pelargoniums are key plants for the summer container garden. *P.* 'Irene' is a beautiful coral colour.

TYPE .... Planted ....

Variety .... Flowered ....

Tip for next year ....

TYPE .... Planted ....

Variety .... Flowered ....

Tip for next year ....

TYPE .... Planted ....

Variety .... Flowered ....

Tip for next year ....

TYPE .... Planted ....

Variety .... Flowered ....

Tip for next year ....

TYPE .... Planted ....

Variety .... Flowered ....

Tip for next year ....

TYPE .... Planted ....

Variety .... Flowered ....

Tip for next year ....

TYPE .... Planted ....

Variety .... Flowered ....

Tip for next year ....

TYPE .... Planted ....

Variety... Flowered ....

Tip for next year ....

TYPE .... Planted ....

Variety... Flowered ....

Tip for next year ....

TYPE .... Planted ....

Variety... Flowered ....

Tip for next year ....

TYPE .... Planted ....

Variety... Flowered ....

Tip for next year ....

TYPE .... Planted ....

Variety... Flowered ....

Tip for next year ....

TYPE .... Planted ....

Variety... Flowered ....

Tip for next year ....

TYPE .... Planted ....

Variety... Flowered ....

Tip for next year ....

above The aptly named *Helenium* 'Indianersommer' produces a riot of colour into the autumn.

below Winter hellebores look stunning planted among *Scilla bithynica*.

annuals

above The spring-flowering *Viola* family includes many popular flowers, such as heartsease, sweet-scented violets and pansies.

below Sunflowers and nasturtiums provide vibrant colour in the summer months.

TYPE ....

Variety ....

....

Sown ....

Thinned ....

Tip for next year ....

TYPE ....

Variety ....

....

Sown ....

Thinned ....

Tip for next year ....

TYPE ....

Variety ....

....

Sown ....

Thinned ....

Tip for next year ....

TYPE ....

Variety ....

....

Sown ....

Thinned ....

Tip for next year ....

TYPE ....

Variety ....

....

Sown ....

Thinned ....

Tip for next year ....

TYPE ....

Variety ....

....

Sown ....

Thinned ....

Tip for next year ....

TYPE ....

Variety ....

....

Sown ....

Thinned ....

Tip for next year ....

climbers

TYPE ....

Variety ....

Pruned ....

Planted ....

Flowered ....

Tip for next year ....

TYPE ....

Variety ....

Pruned ....

Planted ....

Flowered ....

Tip for next year ....

TYPE ....

Variety ....

Pruned ....

Planted ....

Flowered ....

Tip for next year ....

TYPE ....

Variety ....

Pruned ....

Planted ....

Flowered ....

Tip for next year ....

TYPE ....

Variety ....

Pruned ....

Planted ....

Flowered ....

Tip for next year ....

TYPE ....

Variety ....

Pruned ....

Planted ....

Flowered ....

Tip for next year ....

TYPE ....

Variety ....

Pruned ....

Planted ....

Flowered ....

Tip for next year ....

above As well as flowers, clematis have lovely fluffy seedheads that last until autumn. This is C. 'Bill Mackenzie'.

below *Passiflora caerulea* sports the most distinctive flowerheads in summer.

trees

above Exotic magnolias, such as *M. campbellii*, make excellent features in the spring garden.

below Dramatic autumn foliage is one of the highlights of the gardening calendar.

TYPE ....

Variety ....

Pruned ....

Planted ....

Flowered ....

Tip for next year ....

TYPE ....

Variety ....

Pruned ....

Planted ....

Flowered ....

Tip for next year ....

TYPE ....

Variety ....

Pruned ....

Planted ....

Flowered ....

Tip for next year ....

TYPE ....

Variety ....

Pruned ....

Planted ....

Flowered ....

Tip for next year ....

TYPE ....

Variety ....

Pruned ....

Planted ....

Flowered ....

Tip for next year ....

TYPE ....

Variety ....

Pruned ....

Planted ....

Flowered ....

Tip for next year ....

TYPE ....

Variety ....

Pruned ....

Planted ....

Flowered ....

Tip for next year ....

conifers

TYPE ....

Variety ....

....

Planted ....

Pruned ....

Tip for next year ....

TYPE ....

Variety ....

....

Planted ....

Pruned ....

Tip for next year ....

TYPE ....

Variety ....

....

Planted ....

Pruned ....

Tip for next year ....

above Dwarf conifers planted close will gradually merge with one another to create a living sculpture.

TYPE ....

Variety ....

....

Planted ....

Pruned ....

Tip for next year ....

below Conifers, including pines, spruces and junipers, offer interesting foliage forms and colours. This is *Picea pungens* 'Hoopsii'.

TYPE ....

Variety ....

....

Planted ....

Pruned ....

Tip for next year ....

TYPE ....

Variety ....

....

Planted ....

Pruned ....

Tip for next year ....

TYPE ....

Variety ....

....

Planted ....

Pruned ....

Tip for next year ....

index

Page numbers in *italic* refer to the illustrations

below *Fritillaria meleagris.*

above *Camassia* with buttercups.

above *Bougainvillea.*

below *Allium cristophii* and *Salvia sylvestris* 'Lye End'.

above Shrubs under a blanket of snow.

below Viburnum flowers add colour to a winter garden.

acknowledgements

The publisher would like to thank the following for their assistance:
Bilboul Gardens, Earl's Terrace, London, designed by Bowles and Wyer; Diana Boston, The Manor, Hemingford Grey, Cambridgeshire; Bosvigo House, Cornwall (page 170b); Beth Chatto; Dartington Hall, Devon (Dartington Hall Trust); The Dillon Garden, Dublin (pages 126–7); Fardel Manor, Devon; Great Dixter, East Sussex; The High Beeches, West Sussex (High Beeches Gardens Conservation Trust); Ilford Manor (page 228tl); Liz Middlebrook, The Garden House, Buckland Monachorum (pages 158–9); RHS Rosemoor, Devon (pages 174–5); Mrs. J. Smith, Edmonsham House, Edmonsham, Wimbourne, Dorset (pages 100–1, 116–17) – call 01725 517207 to confirm opening hours; Dr Anthony Steven, Fardel Manor, Devon (pages 106, 114); The Stone-market Garden, RHS Tatton Park 2001 designed by Geoffrey Whiten (page 171t); Westonbirt Arboretum, Gloucestershire (Forestry Commission); Sumil Wickes' Garden designed by Lara Copley-Smith (pages 130–1, 170t); RHS Wisley.

The publisher would also like to thank the following for permission to reproduce their pictures:
Jonathan Buckley: pages 220t, 221tr, 228b Ketley's, East Sussex; 229bl Chelsea Flower Show 1999; 232–3 Glen Chantry, Essex. The Garden Picture Library: pages 132bl, 137tr, 200bl, 203tl © Jerry Pavia; 134tl, 135r, 144tc, 195tc © Howard Rice; 134tc, 199tc © Neil Holmes; 135tr, 146br, 224, 225br © JS Sira; 147br © Clive Nichols; 149bc, 152bl, 203br © Mark Bolton; 166tl © Steven Wooster; 167, 208bl © Meyer/Le Scanff; 173, 190br, 200bl, 201tr, 209bl © John Glover; 203bl © Philippe Bonduel; 207bc © Didier Willery; 209br © Rachel White; 223tr © Marie O'Hara; 225tr © Brigitte Thomas. David Markson: pages 187t and 199br, 201br, 220bl, 221b. All other photographs © Anness Publishing Limited.